COPING WITH OCD

practical strategies for living well with obsessive-compulsive disorder

BRUCE M. HYMAN, PH.D., LCSW
and TROY DUFRENE

New Harbinger Publications, Inc.

Publisher's Note

This publication is designed to provide accurate and authoritative information in regard to the subject matter covered. It is sold with the understanding that the publisher is not engaged in rendering psychological, financial, legal, or other professional services. If expert assistance or counseling is needed, the services of a competent professional should be sought.

Distributed in Canada by Raincoast Books

Copyright © 2008 by Bruce Hyman and Troy DuFrene
New Harbinger Publications, Inc.
5674 Shattuck Avenue
Oakland, CA 94609
www.newharbinger.com

Cover design by Amy Shoup; Text design by Michele Waters-Kermes; Acquired by Catharine Sutker; Edited by Nelda Street

Printed in the United States of America

Library of Congress Cataloging-in-Publication Data

Hyman, Bruce M.
  Coping with OCD : practical strategies for living well with obsessive-compulsive disorder / Bruce M. Hyman and Troy DuFrene.
      p. cm.
  Includes bibliographical references.
  ISBN-13: 978-1-57224-468-9 (pbk. : alk. paper)
  ISBN-10: 1-57224-468-2 (pbk. : alk. paper) 1. Obsessive-compulsive disorder--Popular works. I. DuFrene, Troy, 1972- II. Title.
  RC533.H947 2008
  616.85'227--dc22
                        2008012127

10   09

10   9   8   7   6   5   4   3   2

Two professional secrets: First, cognitive behavior therapy (CBT) is more effective than medications for OCD in both short- and long-term benefits, and second, exposure and ritual prevention, the effective elements in CBT, must be done by OCD patients themselves. With these secrets revealed, how can OCD sufferers obtain CBT? Ideally, by finding an expert cognitive behavior therapist to guide their therapy. Since expert therapists are in very short supply, patients can also use Coping with OCD *to close the gap between what is known and available.* Coping with OCD *provides excellent specific guidance so OCD patients can carry out CBT themselves. It is a welcome addition to the armamentarium of OCD treatments and Hyman and DuFrene are to be commended for writing it.*

> —John Greist, MD, distinguished senior scientist at the Madison Institute of Medicine, clinical professor of psychiatry at the University of Wisconsin, and director of Healthcare Technology Systems

Coping with OCD *is a timely, informative, and readable book on obsessive-compulsive disorder, the "doubting disease". The authors give practical advice on understanding the causes of OCD, and changing the way that sufferers accept, reframe and refocus their thoughts so that they can live life in the present, maintain their progress, and get the most out of life in spite of the OCD.*

> —Eric Hollander, MD, Esther and Joseph Klingenstein Professor and Chair of Psychiatry and director of the Seaver and New York Autism Center of Excellence at Mount Sinai School of Medicine

OCD is a common, painful, and often disabling disorder. People with OCD are tortured by intrusive thoughts and struggle with compulsive efforts to find peace of mind. The treatment of choice for OCD is cognitive behavior therapy. The standard treatment has been based on behavioral work using exposure to obsessions and refraining from compulsions. Cognitive behavior therapy is a living discipline, and in recent years exciting new ideas have formed what is known as the third wave. These ideas, in the form of acceptance and commitment therapy and mindfulness practice blend with exposure-based treatment to offer a powerful new way to separate the suffering from the experience of obsessions. There is a Buddhist saying that pain is inevitable but suffering is optional. Hyman and DuFrene have skillfully blended the third wave with proven exposure-based therapy into an accessible guide to coping with OCD. They describe the path away from suffering.

—James Claiborn, Ph.D, ABPP, psychologist with a practice specializing in OCD in Maine, founding fellow of the Academy of Cognitive Therapy and member of the Scientific Advisory Board of the Obsessive-Compulsive Foundation

This book is the next best thing to private sessions with one of the country's best OCD therapists. Whether you're in treatment for OCD or not, reading this book will be worth many hundreds of dollars to you. It's packed with useful advice for everyone with OCD, including effective new treatment techniques.

—Bruce Mansbridge, Ph.D., director of the Austin Center for the Treatment of OCD

Coping with OCD *joins the highest tier of other patient-focused OCD books. People with OCD (and their loved ones) will appreciate the easy-to-read and practical nature of the text. Hyman and DuFrene provide numerous insights and directions for challenging OCD symptoms that may help the reader learn how to think and act differently and ultimately gain greater control of his or her condition.*

—Eric A. Storch, Ph.D., assistant professor and director of Cognitive Behavioral Therapy Research in the Departments of Psychiatry and Pediatrics at the University of Florida

This book brings Hyman's expert knowledge and clinical wisdom to OCD sufferers and their families with clarity and compassion. Built on the latest scientific evidence, it incorporates the latest standards and directions in the treatment of OCD. Very easy to read, it tackles the bewilderment and pain that OCD brings and makes the complexities of OCD and its treatment quickly understandable. Full of practical and powerful strategies, this exceptional book will be a valuable resource for any OCD sufferer or family member. It brings sufferers hope, optimism and empowerment to take control of their lives in spite of OCD. I will recommend it with enthusiasm!

—Aureen P. Wagner, Ph.D., clinical associate professor of neurology at the University of Rochester School of Medicine and Dentistry, director of the Anxiety Wellness Center in Rochester, NY, member of the scientific advisory board of the Obsessive-Compulsive Foundation, and author of *What to Do When Your Child Has OCD* and *Treatment of OCD in Children and Adolescents: A Professionals' Kit*

This is a timely and welcome addition to the self-help literature for OCD sufferers. The authors offer a straightforward and user-friendly guide to the latest approaches in treatment, integrating newer acceptance and mindfulness approaches with the tried-and-true cognitive behavior techniques that have proven so effective. The book is well written with an engaging style that communicates warmth, humor, and compassion. I will recommend it to my patients and others who suffer from OCD and to therapists who wish to refresh their thinking about OCD and its treatment.

—Charles S. Mansueto, Ph.D., member, Scientific Advisory Board of the Obsessive Compulsive Foundation and director of the Behavior Therapy Center of Greater Washington

This book is dedicated to those who struggle with obsessive-compulsive disorder and their loved ones. May your efforts be rewarded with hope, freedom, and a rich and purposeful life.

Contents

The Doubting Disease

It's a typical morning. You're moving through the house, getting ready to leave for the day. You go from room to room, double-checking the latches on the windows. "Are all the burners on the stove turned off? What about the iron?" You'd better make sure.

You're already out on the front step when a thought hits you: "Is the back door locked?" Dashing through the house, you find the dead bolt in place, but you flip the latch a couple of times anyway—just to be sure. Back at the front door, you turn your key in the lock, and you're ready to go. You start the car and make it as far as the stop sign at the end of the block before the doubting starts:

"Is the back door locked?"

"Did I turn off the stove?"

"What about the bedroom window?"

You remember securing the house, but you just can't shake the unsettling feeling that you forgot to do something important. An intruder could slip in through an unlocked window or door. In no time at all, a burner you left on could incinerate the house. It'll just take a minute, you figure, so you go back and check—just to be sure.

On checking again, you find all the doors and windows locked. The stove and iron are off and feel cool to the touch. Once again you drive away, but before you even make it to the stop sign, the doubts return, stronger than ever. Something could be very wrong.

You circle the block, park the car, and go back into the house. Nothing has changed. You feel a little silly as you touch each of the knobs on the stove, feeling the little arrows that point to the off position—just to be sure. You move from window to window, feeling the latches—just to be sure. When you relock the front door, you turn your key three times, grab the door handle, and rattle it—just to be sure.

But as you drive away, that ache in the pit of your stomach returns with a wrenching sense of uncertainty, fear, and dread. Your mind races; you mull over the events of the past few minutes again and again, trying to reassure yourself. But it's not enough. You need to go back and check again—just to be sure.

You find everything exactly as you left it, all in order. "I must be crazy," you mutter. You're already running late for work as you get into the car for the fourth time. You manage to stifle your racing mind long enough to make it past the stop sign, but the gnawing, unsettling doubts dog you all day long.

And they reappear the next morning and the next—week after week, year after year.

If this frustrating experience sounds all too familiar, you may be struggling with *obsessive-compulsive disorder*, or OCD. Psychologists and psychiatrists classify OCD within a group of mental health problems known as *anxiety disorders*. The symptoms of all the anxiety disorders vary widely. However, taken as a whole, anxiety disorders are among the most common mental health problems by a wide margin.

Getting to Know OCD

OCD is a complex condition with a wide variety of symptoms, so your OCD may manifest itself very differently from the scenario you just read. However, there are two elements common to all forms of OCD. As you probably guessed from the name of the disorder, these two elements are called *obsessions* and *compulsions*.

- **Obsessions** are persistent, unwanted thoughts, feelings, or impulses that intrude on your mind. They usually incorporate themes of potential harm or danger to yourself or, more often, to others. Obsessions cause excessive anxiety, worry, and doubt.

- **Compulsions** are mental acts or repetitive behaviors you perform in an attempt to relieve or prevent the anxiety, worry, or doubt caused by your obsessions. You may feel that your compulsive behaviors have a seemingly magical power to prevent or avert dreaded events such as death, illness, or some other feared misfortune.

Obsessions and compulsions are often interrelated. Obsessions usually begin with persistent doubt, which is why OCD is sometimes referred to as "the doubting disease." In the story that began this chapter, no matter how hard you tried, you still doubted that the stove was off, the doors were locked, and so forth. This doubt leads to intolerable levels of uncertainty, which generates anxiety. To relieve the anxiety, you may start engaging in compulsive behavior—excessive washing, checking, reassurance seeking, and so forth. These behaviors might relieve your anxiety for a little while, but the relief won't last long. The anxiety-provoking obsession returns, often stronger and more frequently than before. So you may try to adopt even more elaborate rituals to relieve the anxious feelings of uncertainty.

Do you see where this leads? Obsessions and compulsions combine to create a vicious cycle, each provoking and worsening the other. In its milder forms, the cycle of obsession and compulsion can be annoying and inconvenient. At its most extreme, it can be severely disruptive to all aspects of your life, resulting in total disability.

As long as obsessions and compulsions are a significant part of the problems you're experiencing, you probably have OCD. But as previously mentioned, there are many varieties of the disorder. Here are some of the most common:

- **Compulsive checking:** The story that began this chapter was an example of this kind of OCD. Sufferers repeatedly check objects such as doors, locks, and household appliances, fearing pending disaster if they are not checked and rechecked, then checked again.

- **Compulsive washing and cleaning:** This type of OCD is characterized by persistent worrying about contamination from dirt, germs, or foreign substances and living with the constant dread of either being harmed or causing harm to others. People struggling with this compulsion may frequently wash, clean, or overuse sanitizing chemicals on their bodies or within their home environments to relieve these worries.

- **Compulsive ordering and symmetry obsessions:** People with this kind of OCD feel compelled to arrange certain items or carry out tasks repeatedly until they feel "just right." They can become extremely distressed if objects they've arranged are moved, touched, or rearranged or if their ordering tasks are not carried out perfectly.

- **Pure obsessions (also known as *primarily obsessional OCD*):** In this form of OCD, unwanted violent or sexually inappropriate thoughts and images intrude upon the mind of the sufferer. These OCD sufferers intensely fear losing control and endangering either themselves or their loved ones. People who have this form of OCD struggle to actively suppress the unwanted thoughts and avoid situations in which they are likely to occur. Some people with this form engage in repetitive thoughts such as counting, praying, or repeating certain words to neutralize anxiety. (See chapter 4 for information specifically about primarily obsessional OCD.)

- **Hoarding:** A form of OCD that gets more than its share of attention in the news and popular culture, hoarding involves collecting insignificant items and experiencing difficulty discarding things that most people consider to be junk, for example, old newspapers and magazines, milk cartons, and even cigarette ashes. Hoarding can endanger the health, safety, and normal functioning of those suffering from it.

- **Scrupulosity:** This religious form of OCD involves persistent worry about possibly insulting or offending God by violating religious rules or principles. This form of compulsion may prompt sufferers to pray or confess excessively, or seek frequent reassurance, especially from the clergy, about their own moral purity.

- **Health-related OCD:** Characterized by persistent worries about the possibility of being or becoming ill with a catastrophic disease, this compulsion may involve repeatedly checking the body for signs of disease and making frequent trips to doctors and hospitals for reassurances of good health.

What's It Like Living with OCD?

If you have OCD, you're probably very concerned about whatever "bad" thoughts you may have, feeling very guilty about and overwhelmingly responsible for them. To you, thinking about a violent or inappropriate act might seem the same as actually committing it. Your thoughts about some disaster or misfortune might feel like a strong portent that the event will actually happen unless you act to prevent it.

If you regard your thoughts as powerful indicators of what might or might not happen—and you frequently have disturbing thoughts—you're left in a very difficult position. Some people say this feels like walking through a field of land mines. Your thoughts constantly warn you that danger lurks at every turn. You live in almost constant fear of those dangers and never know where or when you'll stumble on one of these hidden mines, but all it takes is one misstep and—kaboom!—you are overwhelmed with fear that your worst nightmare is about to come true. To control the sense of danger and accompanying anxiety, you resort to rituals and behaviors that you think might protect you from these mines, allowing you to go about your business with less worry.

Does this sound familiar? It should. It's yet another take on the vicious cycle of obsessions and compulsions that you just read about. Your rituals might temporarily disable the mines, giving you a few minutes of short-lived relief. But sooner or later you'll have to cross that field again, and the mines will be back—and there will likely be more of them, with shorter fuses and more powerful charges than before.

Another characteristic of the disorder is this: If your obsessive concerns are with possible harm or danger to yourself or others, even the slightest degree of uncertainty about the risks involved will trigger enormous fear and dread. You may react to the lottery-like odds of this or that catastrophe actually happening as if it were as certain as death and taxes. To prevent danger from coming to pass, the brain-circuitry glitch of OCD makes you struggle to do things just right, without the remotest possibility of error, miscue, or imperfection. Consequently you may approach everyday tasks that people without OCD carelessly breeze through—grooming, laundry, navigating the city streets—with over-meticulous and time-consuming care. But the forty-five minutes you take to floss your teeth or the two hours you take to drive around the block likely baffles, confuses, and angers those close to you. Of course, such reactions from others can leave you feeling isolated and alone, making the experience of OCD even more painful and frustrating for you.

Who Gets OCD and Why?

OCD occurs on every continent, in every society, and at every level of social and economic class. If you think you might have OCD, you're in good company: about one person in forty suffers from the disorder (Yaryura-Tobias and Neziroglu 1997). Its symptoms can appear at any point within the life cycle but most commonly begin during childhood, adolescence, or young adulthood. Many people with OCD experience their first symptoms during childhood, as repetitive touching, tapping, or counting behaviors; obsessions with dirt, germs, or "the cooties"; or persistent and repetitive demands for reassurance from their parents. Onset of OCD in childhood generally predicts a lifelong predisposition to the problem.

Although many theories exist, and new and promising research is always in progress, the cause of OCD is not currently known. During the early twentieth century, OCD was considered to be the result of bad parenting, specifically inadequate toilet training, but this theory is universally rejected today. The most compelling evidence we now have suggests that the disorder is caused, at least in part, by inherited, genetically transmitted tendencies toward dysfunctions of brain chemistry and circuitry that render the individual vulnerable to developing the disorder. Factors in our environments, specifically having overly worrisome parents or experiencing early childhood stressors such as parental death, illness, and divorce may also contribute to a vulnerability to OCD symptoms. Indeed, OCD seems to result from a complex interaction between genetic and environmental factors.

Diagnosing OCD

So, how do you know if you have OCD? For a mental health professional to formally diagnose you with the disorder, your reoccurring obsessions and compulsions must cause you marked distress, consume hours of time every day, and cause significant impairment in your daily work and family activities. Also, it is key to the diagnosis of OCD that at some point during the course of your experiencing these symptoms, you recognize that the obsessions or compulsions are excessive, unreasonable, or even silly.

It is also possible to have less severe, or subclinical, levels of OCD. This means that you may experience certain OCD symptoms, but they are less disruptive and disturbing to you than the clinical criteria describe. You can lead a normal life despite such low-level symptoms, but you may be vulnerable to significant flare-ups of your symptoms at certain times. Life transitions, family illnesses, moving, changing jobs, marriage, divorce, and becoming a parent for the first time can all drive moderate symptoms to a more severe and impairing level. Biological factors may also play a role. For example, among women, even normal hormonal changes associated with the menstrual cycle and pregnancy can aggravate OCD. Ironically, your symptoms may be at their worst during periods of newly found success, prosperity, and accomplishment—those moments when you grab life's brass ring. It's at these times when your habitual "What if...?!" thinking renders you painfully aware of how much you now have to lose in your career, family relationships, stature, and self-image.

Even if your symptoms fall short of a clinical OCD diagnosis, your experiences with obsessions and compulsions can be painful and disheartening, and may lead to more significant problems later on. Down the road you'll thank yourself for learning how to take care of them now. Reading this book is a great place to start.

What OCD Is Not

So, you have obsessive thoughts and engage in compulsive behaviors. That means you have OCD, right? Not necessarily. It's important to know that some thoughts and behaviors, while greatly resembling obsessions and compulsions, are actually not related to OCD.

Those with strong religious convictions may pray many times a day, relying on prayer to deepen their religious connection or spirituality. Others may toss salt over their left shoulders and avoid stepping on cracks in the sidewalk to "hedge their bets" and avoid misfortune. But generally, neither prayer nor superstition alone is reason to suspect OCD. Most of us engage in some kind of culturally or religiously prescribed rituals at some time, but unless such behaviors excessively disrupt your life or consume a great deal of your time, they probably don't indicate OCD.

When people abuse alcohol or can't seem to stay away from games of chance, others might refer to them as "compulsive" drinkers or gamblers. But this kind of behavior is very different from the compulsions that figure in OCD. While some of us may feel compelled to drink or use drugs, gamble, or smoke four packs of cigarettes a day, all of these behaviors offer at least some promise of pleasure and satisfaction, even while we may ignore the dire inherent health risks in these behaviors. In contrast, the compulsive behaviors associated with OCD, such as washing, cleaning, or checking, are, at the very least, useless and often downright unpleasant. OCD sufferers perform their rituals to control discomfort and anxiety, not because these behaviors give them any kind of pleasure or gratification. The compulsive behaviors of OCD are not pleasure producing but, rather, are discomfort reducing.

Another condition related to, but not the same as, OCD is called *obsessive-compulsive personality disorder*, or *OCPD*. "Personality" is a catch-all term describing the mental, emotional, and behavioral characteristics that make each of us unique and distinct. However, sometimes individuals' personalities may clash with others' in work, social, and personal relationships. These conflicts can be very pervasive and profound, making it hard or impossible for such individuals to function in life. What's more, the differences can be so essential to these people's view of themselves and the world that they may feel that there is nothing wrong and thus have no inclination to seek help. Psychologists call such a condition a *personality disorder.*

People with OCPD are preoccupied with order, perfection, and control. They may be excessively devoted to work, overly conscientious and scrupulous, and unusually rigid and stubborn. Sometimes they hoard worthless objects or fixate on health-related issues. Generally they live highly predictable, structured, and repetitive lives.

Sounds a lot like OCD, doesn't it? But remember how we described the two essential components of OCD: Obsessions are *unwanted* thoughts that cause anxiety, worry, and doubt; and compulsions are repetitive thoughts and behaviors that attempt to *relieve* the anxiety caused by obsessions. People with OCPD have obsessive thoughts without necessarily being bothered by them. They engage in compulsive behaviors as a matter of course rather than as a means of relieving anxiety. Whereas people with OCD suffer greatly from their symptoms and wish to be rid of them, those with OCPD are usually quite comfortable with their behavior. They are often unaware of how it affects their lives until confronted by others and, even then, are typically unwilling to accept guidance and intervention. With experienced and diligent professional care, it is possible for people with OCPD to change, but often it takes dire circumstances to motivate them to wholeheartedly face their problems.

Treating OCD

The good news is that there is much you can do, on your own and with the help of a qualified professional, to effectively manage OCD, reduce distress, and feel freer to do what is important to you in life. The most effective treatments for OCD currently include medication and cognitive behavioral therapy. For most people, a combination of these two treatments offers the best chances for effective long-term recovery and management of OCD.

The medications most often used to help reduce OCD symptoms are a class of drugs called *serotonin re-uptake inhibitors*, or *SSRIs*. These drugs act to enhance the level of the brain chemical serotonin, a neurotransmitter that helps regulate mood and emotions. Imbalances of serotonin in the brain are thought to play an important role in the severity of OCD symptoms. SSRIs improve OCD symptoms by increasing the levels of serotonin in the brain. In clinical use, these medications relieve symptoms by 30 to 60 percent in most OCD sufferers. While SSRIs are not without side effects, they're relatively well tolerated by most people who take them and are considered safe for long-term use.

The decision to take medications for OCD is one that you should make in consultation with a physician, preferably a *psychiatrist*, a medical doctor who specializes in the pharmacological treatment of mental disorders. It's a good idea to choose a psychiatrist who has experience in successfully treating OCD patients with medication. (For more information about medication as a treatment for OCD, see the suggestions for further reading provided in chapter 8.)

Medication can significantly reduce OCD symptoms, but for most people with the disorder, it's only a partial solution. A form of psychotherapy, specifically *cognitive behavioral therapy*, or *CBT*, is very often necessary for those seeking lasting recovery from their symptoms. The specific approach taken in CBT to relieving OCD is called *exposure and response prevention*, or *ERP*. This is a symptom-focused treatment that effectively breaks the vicious cycle of obsessions and compulsions by helping you learn alternative ways to deal with disturbing thoughts and compulsive urges. ERP is best administered by a psychotherapist who is trained and experienced in its use. It requires a high degree of commitment and courage to be effective, but your diligence and patience will be well rewarded with a significant reduction in your symptoms and increased freedom from OCD. Successful ERP is not a cure for OCD, but this set of powerful cognitive-behavioral tools can help you effectively manage OCD symptoms throughout your life.

Another well-established approach within the realm of CBT includes cognitive therapy. This approach may be useful for those who are too reluctant to induce the levels of discomfort required for successful exposure and response prevention. Instead, cognitive therapy engages the person with OCD in directly challenging the dysfunctional beliefs and ideas that fuel the OCD. Examples of such dysfunctional ideas include:

- "My bad thoughts are a certain predictor of how dangerous I will become in the future."

- "I must be in control of myself and my thoughts at all times; otherwise, terrible harm will come to me and those I care about."

- "If I think a bad thought, I will cause bad things to happen."

- "Only by doing my compulsions can I be assured that I or my loved one is safe."

Cognitive therapy encourages the OCD sufferer to actively challenge these beliefs by critically examining the evidence upon which such beliefs are based. Through a process known as *cognitive restructuring*, belief disputation and the use of behavioral experiments designed to test the validity of these beliefs, the person with OCD can begin to loosen the grip of the vicious cycle of obsessions and compulsions.

Cutting-Edge Approaches to OCD Treatment

Within the relatively young field of cognitive behavioral therapy for OCD are some exciting innovations that may hold promise for patients who may not respond to the more established treatment approaches. These approaches fall under the general category of mindfulness. Mindfulness is defined as a state of detached awareness of one's experience without judgment or reaction (Kabat-Zinn 2003). By becoming more of an observer of your distressing and disturbing thoughts without judging or reacting to them, you can significantly reduce the impact of OCD on your life.

Perhaps the newest and most promising of the mindfulness approaches is called *acceptance and commitment therapy*, or *ACT* (pronounced as a word rather than individual letters).

ACT has been found to be an important step forward in the treatment of a number of mental health challenges, including OCD. More than simply a new technology for therapy, ACT takes a fresh, new look at the nature of mental health. An ACT therapist is likely to be less concerned with whether you "have OCD" and more interested in how you direct and function in your life as a whole. ACT treatments seek to help you achieve greater psychological flexibility in your life by helping you:

- Remain in contact with the present moment rather than engage in constant OCD "fearcasting" about future catastrophic events.

- View yourself as a context in which things happen rather than a rigid set of qualities and conditions that define how your life must be lived.

- Accept your life as it is, without needless struggle.

- Keep from "fusing" with your thoughts, or acting as if they were unalterable facts rather than just words and images occurring in your mind.

- Clarify what you value, what you want your life to be about apart from the endless pursuit of "certainty" that is the hallmark of OCD.

- Commit to acting in ways that make your values come to life.

Some of the approaches and techniques used in ACT will seem very familiar to you if you've had any experience with traditional CBT. Others might seem odd or even disorienting. But research evidence is fast accumulating that suggests that ACT may be effective at helping people let go of problems like OCD and get on with the business of living well. While this is not a book about ACT per se, the ideas underlying ACT are very much evident in these pages, and much of what is written here is consistent with how an ACT approach to OCD might look.

If you're interested in learning more about ACT, please take a look at the reading recommendations in chapter 8. You may also want to keep an eye on some of the informational websites we mention in that chapter for up-to-the-minute developments in the use of ACT to help with OCD. When we were writing this book, significant research about the use of ACT for OCD was in press (Twohig, Hayes, and Masuda; in press). It is likely that books on the subject will be forthcoming in the near future.

How to Use This Book

Coping with OCD is intended to be a companion to both beginners and veterans on the journey toward an effective and purposeful life, lived in spite of the challenges posed by OCD. The book is a good place to begin if you're just starting out in managing your OCD. The short tips and exercises in this book will serve you well in your day-to-day management of symptoms—as boosters that can help you cope with difficult situations or temporary flare-ups. If your symptoms are mild, these short practices may be all you need to keep OCD from interfering in your life.

This book is also a great tool if you're already receiving treatment for OCD. The techniques you'll find here will strengthen and bolster your daily management of OCD, and the book is small enough to carry around in your pocket or purse, allowing you easy access to encouragement and support when you need it.

Another book you should know about, if you don't have it already, is Dr. Hyman's *The OCD Workbook: Your Guide to Breaking Free from Obsessive-Compulsive Disorder* (second edition), written with coauthor Cherry Pedrick. This more comprehensive book offers a step-by-step approach to managing OCD symptoms. It guides you all the way from the first steps of assessing OCD to preventing relapses after you've achieved control. It also contains invaluable information about how to seek out and make the most of professional treatment if and when you deem it appropriate for your unique situation. If you've already read *The OCD Workbook*, you'll still benefit from the all-new information in *Coping with OCD*. But if you haven't explored it yet, you should definitely consider checking out the workbook when you're ready to learn and do more to manage OCD.

Accepting Your OCD

Picture one of those guys standing on a street corner in ragged clothes, holding up a sign that reads, "The end is near." All day long he prowls around, proclaiming to anyone who'll listen that the killer bees are coming, radio waves cause cancer, nuclear missiles are pointed at our houses, and locusts are poised to swarm over the city. Let's call this fellow "the Doomsayer."

Having OCD is like having this character living in your head. At any moment, he can step out of the shadows to warn you that you could be in danger or that you might be responsible for harming yourself or the people you love and care about most. The Doomsayer seems to know your deepest fears and apprehensions at every moment in your life. He can make you doubt things that you thought you knew about yourself and the world around you. He's persistent, he's crafty, and he's with you every moment of the day.

Intellectually, you realize, at least some of the time, that the dangers depicted by the Doomsayer are overblown nonsense. But he speaks with such conviction, power, and force that you find it impossible to dismiss, diminish, or rationalize away his warnings. When he shows up with his latest foreboding sign and starts reminding you of all the things that can go wrong at any moment in your life, you feel powerless to ignore him. You have grave doubts. Your heart races, your pulse quickens, and your breath shortens. And the only things that seem to diminish his power over you, even a little bit, are your compulsive behaviors and rituals.

So you start washing, cleaning, checking, arranging, avoiding, undoing, or seeking reassurance. But you're trapped. The more you engage in these compulsive behaviors, the more persistent the Doomsayer gets, and the stronger your doubts become. You know these behaviors make no sense, even that they are ridiculous. But you engage in them anyway, anticipating just a few moments of relief. You trade away more and more of your life to ward off your uncomfortable thoughts. After a while, you start to worry whether or not you're getting your rituals just right. That's when the Doomsayer starts to point out to you that, if you don't perform them perfectly, you'll be in trouble—big trouble.

Now, before we go on, we should mention that having the Doomsayer in your head is not the problem. Everyone has to deal with him at some point. Even if it were possible to get rid of him entirely (and it's probably not), you would have to expend a great deal of your finite time and energy to do so—resources that would be much better spent on yourself and your loved ones to craft a rich and purposeful life. But you can learn to see him for what he is and respond to him more effectively.

You can find a way to acknowledge and live with him without letting him run your life. That is what this chapter aims to help you do.

Honestly Assessing Your Life with OCD

If OCD has become your own personal Doomsayer, you probably spend a lot of time and energy seeking relief from your doubts. But we think you'll find that such "relief" comes at a steep price.

Take a minute right now and think about what costs you've had to pay in your life because of your compulsive behavior. You may want to write down your thoughts in a journal or notebook. If you're honest with yourself, this exercise will be hard for you. Here are some things to think about:

- How have compulsive behaviors affected your relationships, your job or profession, and the important roles you play in the lives of people you care about?

- Are you consistently late to appointments and social engagements?

- Do you recruit your family members to participate in your compulsions?

- Is your behavior setting a poor example for your children?

- Are you stressed from having to live a lie, a parallel secret life that hides your compulsions from your friends and loved ones?

- Have you sold out some of your most cherished life goals and dreams due to your OCD?

As you work through these feelings, you'll probably find them pretty painful. Go ahead and let yourself feel that pain. If you can, try to imagine how your loved ones also feel hurt as they helplessly watch you struggle with your compulsions. You may feel quite guilty about the way your OCD has hijacked your life and the lives of the people you care about. It's okay for you to feel guilt and anything else, painful or otherwise, that emerges from this exercise. Just allow it to happen. From this perspective, you now have the opportunity to begin to ask yourself, perhaps for the first time, "How can I use this pain to transform my OCD?"

Pain: Rocket Fuel for Change

Allowing yourself to acknowledge the pain you feel in connection to your OCD can be a strong motivator for change. It can act like rocket fuel, powering your shift from a life dominated by OCD fears and behaviors to one that is rich, purposeful, and rewarding—even *with* the symptoms of OCD.

Let us repeat that: you *can* live an extraordinary life *with* OCD! Having the Doomsayer of OCD in your head may not be the most pleasant experience, but it's just an experience that you have. It doesn't define who you are or what you can become, and it doesn't bar you from living life according to your values. But ironically and paradoxically, to rid your life of the most toxic influences of OCD, you must first acknowledge its presence in your life. The best way to quiet the Doomsayer is to do the seemingly impossible and unspeakable: make friends with him.

Embracing the Doomsayer

"What?!" you gasp. "This OCD is ruining my life, and now you want me to embrace it?!" The simple answer is, well, yes. We do.

It's easy to see OCD as something that happens *to* you, to think of yourself as a victim of the Doomsayer in your head. But to effectively use the pain of OCD as a tool for transforming your life, you must be ready and willing to give up your role as a victim. You must decide that, while you may be hassled or even tormented by the Doomsayer, you're not going to continue to be his victim, and you're not going to sacrifice your whole life to avoid having to listen to his frequent and catastrophic pronouncements. Most importantly, you need to accept that your experience of OCD is not inevitable. No matter what has happened in your past, you need not suffer with OCD.

There is a common metaphor in acceptance and commitment therapy (ACT) that may help you understand this a little more clearly. Imagine that your life right now is a chess game (Hayes and Smith 2005). How would you describe your role in the game?

Maybe you control the white pieces and pawns while the Doomsayer plays the black side. Each move you make takes your life in a direction you want to go, but the Doomsayer is right there, ready to make the next move, pinning you down and keeping you from developing your game as you choose. If you look at the game this way, you might imagine that you're struggling with OCD for control of your life. If you can just figure out the right combination of good tactics and sound strategy, you might be able to get the better of the Doomsayer, to get rid of him once and for all.

Or maybe you see yourself as just one piece on the board—a nervous knight hopping around from square to square, trying to keep himself out of harm's way. In this scenario, instead of squaring off against OCD, you're just blown around the board by forces totally beyond your control.

But there is still a third way that you can imagine your role in this chess game, and it might be a way of looking at the situation that has never occurred to you. What if you're not pieces or pawns at all? What if you're the board itself? There you lie, quietly taking in all the bluster above you, while the white pieces do their dance with the black ones. You encompass it all and provide the context in which the game unfolds. To paraphrase Walt Whitman, you are large; you contain multitudes (Whitman 2005). There's no reason for you to scheme against or defend one side or the other. Everything that happens on the board is a part of you. It's yours to watch unfold. The Doomsayer is a part of you. He's yours to do with as you please. You can hang onto his every word or acknowledge him and wait for him to fall silent on his own.

Now, we're not implying that this realization will be easy or immediate. And we know that the process of change can be both uncomfortable and scary. But take comfort in the thought that many others have gone ahead of you on this path and made real and lasting progress toward a richer life. And there are people out there who can help if the journey seems too much for you. But recognizing that you need not struggle with OCD is the first step toward letting it go and moving on with your life.

Pain vs. Suffering

While having OCD may be painful indeed, suffering with OCD is optional. In fact, pain and suffering are two very different things.

Everyone experiences both physical and psychological pain throughout life. It's unavoidable. We come into the world screaming and leave it in tears and sadness. In fact, you can think of pain as a natural consequence of being alive.

However, suffering is something else entirely. The word "suffer" comes from a Latin root that means "to carry." When you carry around painful experiences long after the initial cause is gone, and subsequently spend excess energy and time avoiding that pain, you open the door to suffering. If you're walking along one day and a golf ball hits you in the head, it will hurt. You'll feel pain. The natural, appropriate response to this pain is to leave one eye open for flying golf balls whenever you are on a golf course. But if you then become intent and resolute that an errant golf ball must never, ever, under any circumstance in your lifetime, fly out of the sky and smack into your skull, you'll invite suffering. And even though the chances of being flattened by another stray drive are lower than your odds of getting struck by lightning, you invite suffering into your life by staying mad at the golf ball that hit you, angry at yourself for having been in the pathway of the golf ball in the first place, and resentful of the golfer who hit it. And you certainly invite suffering into your life when, as many people with OCD might do in this situation, you even avoid at all costs wearing the color green to keep from reminding yourself of golf courses!

While getting hit by a golf ball is a form of pain that pales in comparison with the horrific ideas and images generated by OCD, the suffering caused by OCD evolves in much the same way. By wishing that pain and discomfort were not a part of life, by living a life dedicated to the avoidance of pain, risk, and uncertainty at all costs, your life gets smaller and smaller, and worry and anxiety become your constant companions.

Having OCD vs. Suffering from It

It's easy for you to experience certain kinds of pain, especially if you endure them frequently, as "awful" or "totally unacceptable." However, if you decide that some painful experience is intolerable in your life, you may start wishing never to experience it. You may start avoiding any situation or thought that even remotely might lead to this "awful" kind of pain.

Yes, having OCD sucks. The very real social stigma attached to OCD brings unnecessary isolation and shame. The fact that little is truly known and understood about OCD, and that effective treatment may not be readily available to you, can make having OCD very tough indeed. But the daily act of wishing that you didn't have OCD and wallowing in self-pity over it is guaranteed to increase the extent of your suffering from it. The wishing itself can become yet another obsession. In its worst form, wishing can lead to a sense of powerlessness over your OCD and become a serious detriment to effectively managing it in your life. (Thanks to Dr. Jon Grayson for elucidating the role of the wishing compulsion in the lives of OCD sufferers [Grayson 2004].)

So what do you do instead of wishing you didn't experience OCD? You can embrace it. Or, even better, learn to say thank you to it!

Thank You, OCD!

"What?!" you may well demand. "First I have to embrace OCD, and now I have to be thankful for it? It makes me miserable. What about OCD could I possibly be thankful for?"

We're glad you asked. It's really all just a matter of perspective. You can think of OCD as a pox, a curse, or a terrible stigma that you have to drag around like a ball and chain. Or you can think of it as just another part of your life, as one of the things that makes you a unique and interesting individual.

What are some of the things that OCD can give you?

- When you are not immersed in your OCD, you may actually be much more inclined than most to treat others with compassion. Because you have experienced human suffering firsthand, you can empathize with the suffering of your fellow man. If there is one thing this world needs, it's more heart, more capacity to hear and respond to human suffering. Your enhanced compassion can be a real gift for you and for the people you touch in life.

- You may be very careful, organized, and detail oriented. You're unlikely to make many mistakes, miss a deadline, or get caught by the fine print of an agreement. If you have a job to do, your inclination to pore over details will probably ensure that all the angles will be covered.

- Because you are more likely to value certainty, sameness, and predictability in life over excitement, variety, and stimulation, you can make a terrific partner or employee. If your symptoms do not get in the way too much, you're typically considered someone who is reliable and dependable—someone whom people can really trust. (Of course, the downside is, when your symptoms are bad, you may become grossly unreliable and undependable.)

- Having OCD means that you will persevere at a task for minutes, hours, even days to get it done "just right." No one needs to worry that you will lose interest in a project or cause.

- You are the last person to bend or break rules. It is virtually unthinkable that you'll run afoul of the law or spend any time behind bars.

- You are probably smart. We mean *really* smart. It takes serious mental horsepower to anticipate real or imagined dangers many steps in advance, or to plan the ingenious means necessary to perform the various compulsions and rituals that are a big part of your life. It takes lots of savvy to cajole reassurance from the people around you! Even experienced OCD doctors and therapists inadvertently accommodate people with OCD who are intent upon getting their "reassurance fix."

Boy, This Is Soooo Embarrassing!

If you're like most people with OCD, you regard obsessions and compulsive behaviors as your deep, dark secret. You probably refrain from sharing your OCD experience with any but the most trusted people in your life. In fact, even your most intimate friends and loved ones may not know about your OCD. It's not unusual for people you're very close to, and even those who've known you for a long, long time, to be totally in the dark about the pain you experience. While not naturally prone to deception, dishonesty, or secrecy, OCD sufferers often carry the pain of their OCD deep inside themselves, concealed from those around them, including their loved ones. The keeping of secrets from those closest to you is one of the most painful and burdensome aspects of the disorder.

There are many reasons why you might try to keep your OCD a secret:

- You might consider your obsessive thoughts and compulsive behaviors shameful or embarrassing, even humiliating.

- Whether justified or not, you might fear rejection by your loved ones. You might even imagine that you'll be committed to a mental hospital or have your children taken away if you reveal your OCD to others!

- By keeping your OCD from others, you might feel as if you're protecting them from either the pain of dealing with your OCD or, even worse, from some imagined potential catastrophic harm or danger.

- Though OCD is entirely distinct from psychotic disorders such as schizophrenia, and obsessions clearly differ from the delusions and hallucinations of schizophrenia, you might imagine that the symptoms of your OCD mean you're either "crazy" right now or "going crazy" in the future. (Just for the record, you're not.)

Why Not to Fight Your OCD

Just because we're encouraging you to learn to accept, and even embrace, your OCD doesn't mean we want you to be passive about it. Acceptance doesn't mean doing nothing about OCD's negative impact on your present way of living. You have good reason to take a strong, proactive position regarding reducing the strength and frequency of your obsessions and compulsions. But we want to caution you against fighting your feelings.

Thinking about fighting OCD may conjure up images of the Doomsayer again, this time dressed in satin shorts and wearing padded gloves, and snarling at you from the opposite corner of a boxing ring. Adrenaline courses through your veins; your fists and teeth clench. You're vigilant, ready to dodge his punches and land a few of your own. You're either going to get this guy or go down swinging!

Stop! We promise you, this is not the way to go about overcoming your OCD. Most of us hate fighting, and with good reason. You're as likely to get hurt as the other guy, and you might end up in jail or named the defendant in a nasty lawsuit. And living your life ever ready for a fight is a great way to end up in the cardiac ward. Blow for blow, all of your struggling will get you right back to where you started; only then you'll be too exhausted and worn out to do anything to actually change your life.

But you won't make any progress by doing nothing, either. The eleventh edition of *Merriam-Webster's Collegiate Dictionary* has another definition for "fight." This one reads, "To put forth a determined effort." This kind of fighting can actually do you some good. When you put forth a determined effort to reduce your experience of OCD, you embrace a set of moment-to-moment habits of action and thinking that you commit to applying every day. These habits can keep OCD from getting an edge on you and taking away your ability to live a productive and purposeful life. While not easy, this kind of work will really make a difference. Here are some things to prioritize when starting to retrain your brain to minimize OCD:

- Get to know the nature of your enemy, its habits and patterns.

- Be willing to experience a certain degree of discomfort when you choose to ignore and resist compulsive urges and behaviors.

- Be clear that OCD is a bully that constantly lies to you about the degree of impending danger existing in your life. Because bullies feed on attention, the best way to deal with them is to ignore them.

- Know yourself and your environment. Know when you're strong and when you're weak. Recognize that your OCD "knows" this and will exploit your weakness whenever it can, paralyzing you with fear when you're tired, upset, hassled, or uncertain.

- Learn to be compassionate toward yourself for not being perfect. You may slip from time to time, but your hard work will pay off in the end.

- If you are on medication for OCD, be diligent with your medication regimen. Follow your doctor's recommendations to the letter.

- Build a toolbox of cognitive, behavioral, acceptance, and mindfulness techniques you can use moment to moment throughout the day to deal with OCD flare-ups.

Speaking of tools, let's take a look at some that can really make a difference.

Responding Differently Changes How You Feel

If you've been with us from the beginning of this book, you now have a pretty good handle on what it means (and doesn't mean) to live with OCD. We're going to take it for granted that you're tired of the endless cycle of avoiding risk and discomfort, and the anxiety that comes with it. Are you ready to make a change? Are you ready to find a way out of the OCD trap? We hope so.

This chapter will introduce you to *exposure and response prevention* (*ERP*), a powerful behavior-change strategy for managing OCD. As therapy for OCD, ERP is well supported by more than thirty clinical trials that demonstrate its effectiveness (Abramowitz 1997). A crucial component of successful OCD treatment, it's among the most efficient ways to manage OCD symptoms. ERP is easy to learn but quite challenging to implement. However, if you work at it, it can lead to a significant reduction in your symptoms and an equally significant increase in the control you have over how you live your life.

Talking Back to the Doomsayer

But, before we go on, we want you to understand what you're getting into with ERP. Remember the Doomsayer? When you practice ERP, instead of taking him at his word and running in the other direction, you're going to have a conversation with him. What you'll say depends on what kinds of OCD symptoms you're experiencing. If you have contamination OCD, your conversation might sound something like this:

DOOMSAYER: Hey! Listen here! Don't touch that shopping cart! Do you have any idea how many people touch that thing? And do you know what's on their hands?!

YOU: Yes, I do know that lots of people have touched this cart. But I need to buy groceries, and I can't very well carry them in my arms.

DOOMSAYER: *[surprised by your new reaction]* Er, well... you don't want to get sick, do you? Or infect someone else? All it takes is one germ, you know! What about the bird flu? Hepatitis B? Ebola? How about the AIDS virus?

YOU: Well, I guess there might be a chance that I could catch those things, and I admit that I feel really anxious about it. But I know that the chances are very slim, and I'd rather take the risk of catching something awful than turn a simple ten-minute shopping task into an hour or two ordeal of washing and scrubbing myself, my kids, my car, my groceries, and anything else that may have touched the shopping cart handle. So, if you'll excuse me...

DOOMSAYER: *[stepping aside, stunned]* Hey, what's the matter with you? You usually run back to your car for sanitizing wipes! If you don't, you're going to be exposed for the bad, irresponsible mom/dad you really are and suffer with that guilt for the rest of your life!

YOU: Well, not this time. My heart's pounding now, but I know that the fear will subside soon, if I just wait it out.

DOOMSAYER: *[befuddled]* Hey, did I mention that I saw a kid sneeze on that handle? Right where your hand is!

YOU: *[rolling your eyes]* Yeah, okay. Thanks for warning me, but I have a life to live. See ya around.

ERP essentially involves looking the Doomsayer in the eye and telling him, "I hear what you're saying. I know that I face risks all day long and that I probably can't know *for certain* that something terrible won't happen. But I'm willing to accept that uncertainty and any anxiety that comes with it, and live my life anyway, even when it's uncomfortable for me to do so." From your old OCD viewpoint, this attitude will seem totally confusing, to the point of making no sense at all. In fact, the idea of taking this stance may make you very uncomfortable, but instead of avoiding your fears, you'll face them. Instead of minimizing risk, you'll learn, bit by bit, to take on more and more risks in the service of living a richer, more fulfilling life, free of the most toxic effects of OCD. We won't kid you that it will be easy. It won't. But it will be worth the effort and will gradually get you closer to the life you want to lead.

A Quick but Important Note

ERP is challenging work. Many people with mild to moderate OCD can guide themselves through exposure work on their own with good results. However, some cannot, and people with moderate to severe OCD will likely find the suggestions in this chapter too challenging. Exposure is rarely, if ever, harmful, but if your anxiety is too high to do the work described in this chapter, seek the help of a qualified therapist trained in CBT (see chapter 8 for information on finding a qualified therapist). Those previously diagnosed with a psychotic disorder, such as bipolar disorder or schizophrenia, who are actively abusing substances such as drugs and alcohol or have a history of post-traumatic stress disorder (PTSD) are unlikely to be successful with ERP unless it is conducted under the guidance of a trained and experienced professional.

How Does It Work?

ERP works because of two basic principles, one rooted in the neurological makeup of our brain and the other drawn from theories of learning. The first is the principle of nervous system habituation. Thanks to hundreds of thousands of years of evolution, our survival has been ensured, in part, by the capacity of our nervous and sensory system to respond lightning quick to information in our environment that either poses a threat or keeps us safe. Imagine if, while stopping to enjoy the sweet fragrance of a rose, we found the sensation so long lasting and interminably intoxicating that we failed to notice the hungry saber-toothed tiger sneaking up on us from behind. Our brain evolved such that the sensations processed by it and our sensory system—what we hear, taste, smell, see, and touch—are of a transient nature to prepare us for the next sensory event, an event that could mean the difference between survival and death. As a result, our nervous system is naturally programmed to "numb out" when any one of our senses is exposed to a persistent source of stimulation.

Imagine putting a spoonful of chocolate ice cream in your mouth but being unable to swallow it or spit it out. All you can do is just hold it there. At first, you'll notice the nuanced bittersweetness of the cocoa, the roundness of the vanilla, and the richness of the cream. But after a minute, this exciting and flavorful ice cream will become stale and then bland, finally transforming into tepid and tasteless goo. What happens is that the taste-receptor cells on your tongue are powerfully stimulated when you put the ice cream in your mouth, delivering a "Wow!" sensation to your brain. But as you hold the ice cream in your mouth, your receptor cells become, in a sense, "bored" with the flavor of the ice cream. They send fewer and fewer signals to your brain the longer you hold the stuff in your mouth awaiting the next novel "wow" experience. You basically start to ignore the taste sensations in your mouth.

This neurological phenomenon happens to you all the time, most often without your awareness of it. Think of the sound of your neighbor's lawn mower, the smell of your own cologne or perfume, or the radio playing quietly in the background. After prolonged exposure to particular sense-data, your nervous system stops paying attention to those persistent sources of both pleasurable and painful sensory input.

Certain thoughts, feelings, or situations activate your OCD-related anxiety similarly to the way that food, sound, texture, scents, and light activate your senses. When you do ERP, you remain in *persistent* contact with the thoughts, feelings, or situations that upset you—without escaping from or avoiding them, or resorting to a compulsion or "safety behavior." This prolonged exposure activates the process of habituation. Eventually, as you become habituated to your feared object or situation, you will be less distressed by it.

Another fact of our neurological makeup that assists us in the process of ERP is found in the action of our central nervous system, specifically the autonomic nervous system. This complex pathway of nerves runs throughout the body and is responsible for, among many other things, the activation of the body's response to external threats to our own and our loved ones' survival. Watch your own child chase a baseball out into a busy urban street and you will feel the activation of the sympathetic division of the central nervous system. Our hearts pound, our hair stands on end, our bodies sweat—all in the service of facing and surviving a dangerous situation. Once the threat passes (the child makes it to the other side of the street unharmed), the parasympathetic division of the autonomic nervous system kicks in to shut the original activation down—and have a good talk with that overactive child!

What this means to the person with OCD is that, by doing exposure and staying in the fear-provoking situation without resorting to escape, avoidance, ritual, or other compulsive "safety" behaviors, the parasympathetic system turns off the activation and thus lowers the anxiety without necessitating a compulsive ritual. OCD symptoms persist, in part, because the person overlearns and overrelies upon a dysfunctional habit (for example, repeated hand washing and checking) to shut down the anxiety rather than allow the natural relief provided by our brain and three million years of evolution to automatically shut off the anxiety once the threat has passed.

Exercise: The Polar Bear Trick

Have you ever seen a polar bear shiver? No, because they're all habituated to the cold! This exercise will enable you to really connect with how your body engages in the process of habituation. You may feel silly splashing around in a sink of ice water, but you'll get to really experience how your body reacts to strong stimulation that you choose to engage with rather than avoid. This way, when you get ready to practice ERP with your OCD symptoms, you'll know what kind of results to expect.

1. Fill a sink or large bowl with ice cubes and cover the ice with water.

2. Immerse your hands in the water. For a minute or two, try to avoid giving in to the instinct to pull your hands out of the water.

3. Pay attention to the sensations you feel in your hands.

Well, what did you learn? You probably noticed that, at first, the water felt extremely cold. However, as you continued to hold your hands under the water, you probably sensed the temperature changing. You may have felt nothing at all, or you actually may have felt a warm, or even burning, sensation. After a while, even these secondary sensations also fade from perception. But if you stop and take the temperature of the water, you'll likely find that it's still around 32 degrees, exactly what it was when you initially submerged your hands. The temperature of the water hasn't changed. Instead, your mechanism for perceiving it has changed. Your nerves became "bored" with sensing extreme cold and decided to rededicate themselves to other, more interesting tasks. It is this process that gives ERP much of its power.

ERP: Learning to Tell a False Alarm from a Real Fire

Habituation is one benefit of ERP. Another is that it will allow you to start learning to discern between dangerous situations and those that only seem perilous through the lens of your

OCD. As we explained in chapter 2, OCD involves strong aversion to even the slightest degree of uncertainty about the risk of danger or harm to yourself or others. Many of your "worst-case scenarios"—unknowingly catching a deadly tropical disease from using a public bathroom and then inadvertently passing it to your child, running a school bus off a cliff as you carefully change lanes, losing control and stabbing your loved one with a kitchen knife, or harming someone with your thoughts—are so unlikely that they literally defy statistical forecasting. But you feel very real dread that they might come to pass. Anxiety researchers call these real feelings about all-but-impossible events "false alarms" (Barlow 2004).

Of course, there are some situations that are genuinely dangerous and require a strong, proactive response. If you find yourself standing on the tracks when a train is coming, you'll experience a true alarm. It's both normal and appropriate for you to react strongly to prevent your messy dispatch. On the other hand, the false alarms of fear and dread generated by OCD typically are not about anything as tangible as an oncoming train. The "risks" associated with OCD typically are "What if...?!" dangers that are highly unlikely ever to happen to you, your loved ones, or others! Yet your brain delivers a lightning bolt of fear in response to these "What if...?!" threats as if they were imminent.

If you're sitting in a dark theater and someone shouts "Fire!" you might run for the exit, even if you don't feel heat or smell smoke, just to be on the safe side. You react to a *possible* danger rather than an *actual* one. We all do this from time to time. But when you have OCD, you may find yourself impulsively reacting to possible dangers many times a day, never giving yourself the opportunity to decide whether the alarms are true or false. As you continue to act on these impulses, you'll experience stronger and stronger alarms to even the most harmless of situations. ERP is essentially a process that enables you to directly experience your fear, without escape or avoidance, thereby giving you the opportunity to test your beliefs about which alarms are true and which are false. But to reap the rewards of ERP, first you need to be willing to risk that your worst nightmare may come true. This means accepting risk and uncertainty.

Accepting Risk and Uncertainty

The heart of ERP is a twofold goal that allows you to:

- Let go of your excessive need for control and live more fully, despite the existence of risk and uncertainty.

- Be willing to experience any discomfort associated with these risks and uncertainties so that you can follow through with your life goals.

So far, given your experience with OCD, this has been a problem for you. But we're going to tell you a secret: we're absolutely certain you can accomplish the objective of ERP.

How can we be so sure? Well, you already negotiate a number of genuine risks and their attendant uncertainties every day with confidence and equanimity. But don't take our word for it. Let's look at some numbers, courtesy of the National Safety Council.

Maybe we should forget about the obviously remote odds that, if you go outside, you'll be bitten to death by a snake or lizard (1 in 1,874,034) or struck by lightning (1 in 79,746)—although both mishaps do occur. We'll go out on a limb, though, and assume that you eat from time to time without giving a thought to the fact that your lifetime chance of choking to death on food is 1 in 4,284. Do you shower, bathe, swim, or travel anywhere by boat? Your chances of meeting your end by accidental drowning are 1 in 1,134. Maybe you occasionally climb a ladder, go up on the roof, or hike near boulders and cliffs. Your lifetime odds of perishing in a fall are 1 in 218. Do you drive a car? You have a 1 in 22 lifetime chance of dying in a motor vehicle accident.

How is it possible that you can be perfectly comfortable with so many risky situations in your daily life? It's because you're *willing* to put yourself in a variety of situations *despite* the inherent dangers and risks. Perhaps you left the house today to go shopping; if so, you are taking the risk that someone might have broken in. Or you drove to work today (perhaps not the most pleasurable of experiences), but survived the possibility of becoming a highway statistic in the interest of getting to work on time so that you can pay the bills. Maybe you talked on your cell phone today and decided to risk being exposed to cell phone microwaves, which may (but have been found unlikely to) cause cancer. Maybe you risked failing tests in school to obtain the education you needed to succeed in your life and career. Maybe outdoor sports are your passion, and you wouldn't think twice about taking a run down a ski slope, despite the risks to life and limb, or hotdogging on a surfboard, despite the possible presence of hungry marine creatures.

By your willingness to engage in these "risky" activities, over time you've taught your brain to pay less attention to the potential harm, danger, or failure inherent in them, and more attention to their inherent rewards. Your experience has taught you that it's very useful to engage in these activities because they enable you to live life more fully and enjoyably. In neurological terms, you have habituated to, and even embraced, the uncertainty inherent in these pursuits and activities. You managed to silence the Doomsayer without even realizing you were doing so!

Take a minute to make a list of activities, interests, and pursuits presently untouched by your OCD that others might consider risky, even in some remote way. For example, despite your OCD, you might enjoy driving fast cars! For each activity you list, think about how you learned to be comfortable with it. Perhaps it was out of necessity or because it was pleasurable or fun, or enriched your life in some way. The point here is this: In several ways you've already succeeded to overcome doubt and uncertainty in your pursuit of what's important in your life. So you have already laid the groundwork for your success with ERP. Now, let's get down to the business of actually *doing* ERP.

ERP in Action

As the name implies, there are two steps to ERP. *Exposure* involves initiating direct contact with thoughts, feelings, and impulses in the situations most likely to trigger your anxiety. You can engage with these triggers in the world—say, by touching a doorknob or throwing a piece of old newspaper into the trash. When you do, it's called *in vivo* exposure, because it's something you do "in real life." If you conjure up your triggering situation in your mind's eye—by thinking of a violent or inappropriate thought, for example—the process is called *imaginal* exposure. Depending on the kind of OCD symptoms you experience, in vivo or imaginal exposure (or a combination of both) may be the most effective way for you to engage in ERP.

Response (or *ritual*) *prevention* is the second step of ERP. In this process, you commit to the gradual, though ultimately complete, elimination of those behaviors that you typically use to temporarily reduce or neutralize your anxiety or uncertainty, namely your compulsive rituals and avoidance behaviors. These include both the things you do internally (such as mentally reviewing the past) and externally (such as checking, hand washing, or asking others for reassurance) to increase your sense of safety and reduce the anxiety caused by an obsessive thought.

The Process of ERP

To begin actually doing ERP, we're going to ask you to get out your journal. You do have a journal, don't you? Well, if you don't, no matter. Just find a pencil and paper, and get ready to make a few notes. We'll start by helping you create what therapists call an *exposure hierarchy*. This is a list of anxiety triggers that will help you decide how to begin your exposure work.

Start by identifying various situations, objects, and thoughts that trigger your anxiety and discomfort. Write down each of these. Once you have your list, look it over and assign each situation a score based on the *subjective units of distress* (SUDS), according to the amount of stress that would be generated if you were prevented from engaging in the compulsive behavior you typically use to reduce your anxiety. The SUDS scale is a 100-point, self-reporting measure that you use to indicate the level of distress caused by certain triggers, from least to most severe.

- A state of calm and peace = 0

- A little anxiety and discomfort = 10–30

- Somewhat greater anxiety and discomfort = 40–60

- Extreme anxiety and discomfort = 70–90

- The very worst anxiety or fear you can possibly experience = 100

After you've made your list and given each situation a SUDS rating, go back over the list and rank each situation in order of its SUDS score, with the situation representing the lowest SUDS score at the bottom and the one with the highest SUDS score at the top. At the top should be the situation that represents the most anxiety- and fear-provoking situation you can imagine— a SUDS score of 100. For example, if you have contamination OCD with an obsessive fear of the possibility of contracting the AIDS virus, your list might look like this:

1. Handle a library book titled *The HIV Survival Guide* without washing my hands afterward—100

2. Handle money from a "contaminated" cashier with a slight cut on her forearm without washing afterward—90

3. Buy a newspaper from the homeless person on the busy street corner near my house without washing afterward—80

4. Touch a door handle in a "clean" public washroom without washing afterward—70

5. Touch the tabletop of a "clean" restaurant with my elbow without wiping it with a disinfectant swab afterward—60

It's important that your hierarchy include situations that are sure to trigger your discomfort. For maximum benefit, you should strive to expose yourself daily to situations that generate a minimum level of 60 SUDS. Dr. Fred Penzel, a colleague of Dr. Hyman, puts it this way: "The more discomfort you are willing to experience, the less discomfort you will experience." Put another way, to maximize the benefits of exposure, it is necessary to place yourself in truly uncomfortable situations. Only in this way can you reap the most benefit from ERP.

What your own exposure hierarchy will look like will depend a great deal on what form your OCD takes. Following are just a few examples of what *might* come up for people with a few different kinds of OCD symptoms.

Checking Compulsions

1. Turn off the faucet and walk away without checking that the water has stopped running—100

2. Turn off the stove, checking that the knobs are off just once—90

3. Use the iron, unplug it, and leave the house without checking even once—80

4. Lock the front door of my home just once—70

5. Write a check and seal it in an envelope, reviewing the numbers quickly, just once, then hastily drop it in the mail and walk away—60

Scrupulous or Religious Compulsions

1. Think an "immoral" or "impious" thought on purpose while in my place of worship without confessing or asking for reassurance—100

2. Swat a fly dead without requesting reassurance that this doesn't constitute murder—90

3. Pray imperfectly without being certain of my sincerity—80

4. Pray "imperfectly" without being certain of the meaning of the prayer—75

5. Observe someone sneeze without saying, "Bless you"—70

Ordering Compulsions

1. Place clothes in the closet without arranging by size or color—100

2. Leave some picture frames hanging on the wall with one corner higher than the other without straightening—90

3. Leave dining room chairs placed randomly around the table—80

4. Leave cans of food in the pantry without arranging by contents or size—70

5. Place throw pillows slightly disarranged on the sofa—60

"Just Right" Compulsions

1. Brush my teeth for two minutes (using a timer), then stop before experiencing that "just right" feeling—100

2. Zip up my fly just once, without experiencing that "just right" feeling—95

3. Tie my shoelaces once, getting only a partial "just right" feeling—80

4. Comb my hair for only sixty seconds, then stop before experiencing that "just right" feeling—70

5. Intentionally choose the one necktie that feels "wrong" or "imperfect," and wear it despite my discomfort—60

(For more examples of exposure hierarchies for specific OCD symptoms, see Dr. Hyman's *The OCD Workbook* [New Harbinger 2005] or see chapter 8 for further reading.)

Carrying Out ERP Tasks

Once you've drawn up your exposure hierarchy, start your exposure exercises by focusing on the least-distressing item on the list; however, it is important that the item triggers at least 60 SUDS. Your goal is to expose yourself to this lowest-level trigger for as long as it takes for you to observe your anxiety drop by at least one half. This could take a few minutes, a few hours, or even a few days. What is important is that you immerse yourself as completely as possible in the exposure, without engaging in any kind of compulsion to relieve your anxiety and discomfort. We call this the principle of *total immersion*, which is the best way to harness the powerful effects of habituation to relieve your symptoms.

As you immerse yourself as completely as possible in the exposure experience, try not to do anything to avoid feeling discomfort. Be vigilant about this! You're far more clever than you realize. Avoidance behaviors can be very covert. It's easy to "numb out" during exposures by reassuring yourself that things will be okay. Repeating "mantras" to yourself, such as "I am safe and secure now," is a form of reassurance that will interfere with habituation. So is doing relaxation exercises or pretending that things are other than they are to lessen the anxiety you feel about them. If you touch the trash-can lid, you've got to engage with the idea that it's the lid of a filthy, dirty trash can, which has also been touched by all types of unknown forms of dirt, germs, and putrefaction, rather than pretend that you're touching the lid of, say, a fancy box of chocolates! Remember, the more discomfort you're willing to experience in the service of overcoming your OCD, the better your chances of success with exposure.

To further enhance your encounter with contamination triggers, try the "full body exposure." This will evoke a certain "ugh" response, but it's well worth it. It is done in five steps:

1. Touch a "contaminated" object (such as the door of a public washroom or the inside rim of a trash can) that has a SUDS of at least 60, and rub your hands together so that you feel the contaminant all over your hands.

2. Rub your "dirty" hands up and down your arms (bare arms are best).

3. Reach down and touch your ankles with your "dirty" hands, then slowly move your hands up your calves,

knees, and thighs, followed by your lower and upper torso.

4. Now, touch your hair with your hands (yes, that's right, your clean, freshly washed hair) for three seconds, and then in one motion place your hands on your face, holding it for three seconds.

5. Finally, place a breath mint or piece of hard candy in your "dirty" hand and eat it (yes, you read it right). This completes your full body exposure. You probably are thinking, "That's just too gross!" You're right. It is pretty gross. But just because something is gross, doesn't necessarily make it dangerous or harmful.

Practice this exercise three or four times each day for at least a week. Each day, start the exposure by touching an object just a little more contaminated (higher SUDS rating) than you did the day before. You will be surprised at just how comfortable you become in situations that formerly caused you enormous discomfort. Remember, your goal is to learn to become "comfortable being uncomfortable" and accept the uncertainty about whether or not something horrible will happen. To accomplish this takes time, courage, and practice.

When practicing the principle of total immersion in ERP for contamination issues, it's extremely helpful to spread the "alien" germs and contaminants everywhere in the house. This means that you proceed to touch and therefore contaminate every surface and object in your home with your "filthy" hands, including the kitchen and your clean clothes, sheets, and bedding. While it seems particularly adverse, go ahead and touch objects in your children's rooms (chances are really good that your kids have "survived" touching objects today that are far dirtier than what's on your hands). When you have "contaminated" the entire house, you are done for now. Practice this exposure sequence at least two to three times per day for optimal effect. Again, the goal is total immersion in the situations you fear so that you can achieve habituation.

Of course, as you engage with the things or situations that trigger your anxiety, remember that all of your efforts will be for naught unless you do the response prevention component of ERP. Remember, the defining feature of OCD is the alternation of obsessions with the compulsions that seemingly neutralize doubt, worry, and anxiety. As you expose yourself to your triggering objects and situations, you need to refrain from engaging in compulsions in response to the anxiety. The form of your response prevention will depend on your symptoms. Here is an example of a useful response prevention strategy for contamination OCD with washing compulsions:

> To control your responses, establish strict rules about "legal" and "illegal" washing. A legal wash lasts ten seconds (just about the time it takes to sing rapidly "Happy Birthday to You") and involves using no more than a dime-size dollop of liquid soap (plain, non-antibacterial soap is best). You can engage in a legal wash only once before meals, once after using the toilet, and after getting obvious grease or dirt on your hands. Any other washing is illegal, especially if you're aware that washing would relieve anxiety. Limit your showers to fifteen minutes, once every

other day to start. A brief shower after vigorous exercise constitutes your daily shower. Use only the amount of shampoo, shower gel, and so forth recommended by the manufacturer. Wash each part of your body only once and use a timer to limit the length of your showers. You should feel that you washed "incompletely," and an excellent strategy is to do a full body exposure immediately after your shower (do I hear another "ugh?") "What?" you bark. "That's ridiculous! That will only get me dirty again!" That's exactly correct, and it's what we're striving for. Remember the idea of total immersion discussed earlier? At this point in your ERP, your brain doesn't know the difference between normal clean and OCD clean. So it's best to remain totally immersed, even while repatterning your behavior in the direction of normal (legal) washing and showering. In this way, you will maximize the power of habituation and progress much faster.

(Once again, for more examples of response prevention strategies for specific OCD symptoms, see *The OCD Workbook* [New Harbinger 2005] or chapter 8 for further reading.)

Tips for Better Exposure Practice

- Work up your exposure-hierarchy list gradually, moving to the next item when you've consistently (for two or three days in a row) reduced your preexposure SUDS level by at least half. It is not necessary to eliminate all discomfort prior to moving to a more challenging exposure. What's important is to observe the anxiety go down without the need to engage in a compulsion.

• Remind yourself that, although anxiety may be uncomfortable, it's not dangerous (however, take care to refrain from making this a repetitive habit to relieve discomfort during an exposure).

• Anticipation anxiety about the "unknown" just prior to beginning exposure is normal. Acknowledge it as a normal part of a powerful effort to get your OCD under control.

• Let go of the need to do your exposures perfectly. What's important is the degree to which you are willing to encounter your worst fears while doing the exercises, not how perfectly it goes. If it did not go so well today, there's always another chance tomorrow. Stay positive. Given that most OCD sufferers are extreme critics, let go of the tendency toward excessively criticizing your efforts while doing ERP.

• The journey to recovery does not happen in a straight line. Exposure work involves taking a few steps forward followed by a step backward. Keep focused on your goal—a life with more freedom and possibilities—and stick to it.

- Support from a friend or loved one can be a big help if you choose to do exposure work on your own. If you go this route, choose someone who can be helpful, friendly, and nonjudgmental. People who are too emotionally involved may be unable to offer you the calm, rational support you need to make progress.

- Remember that seeking reassurance from others is a compulsion that must be curtailed for habituation to occur. Your helper must refrain from reassuring you that everything is okay, that nothing bad will happen, or that you will be all right. Treat reassurance as a "drug" that prevents recovery from OCD, by arranging for your helper to gradually withdraw it as you proceed with ERP.

The process of ERP is one that frightens many people with OCD, at least initially. Many people with more severe OCD avoid treatment for years or even a lifetime because they can't stand the prospect of exposing themselves to the things they fear the most. But this doesn't mean that they suffer less; they actually suffer more. No matter how frightening exposure initially seems, it has undoubtedly helped countless numbers of sufferers to live more fully with OCD. It will lead to a reduction of your suffering over time and the exhilaration that true freedom from OCD can bring. If you find that you just can't stand to try this work on your own, we strongly encourage you to seek a qualified professional to help you. Your efforts are likely to be well-rewarded.

My Thoughts Are Driving Me Crazy!

The ERP techniques you read about in chapter 3 (which we hope you're beginning to practice) are some of the best ways you can manage and reduce compulsions, the behavioral aspect of OCD. But the disorder has both a cognitive (what you're thinking) and a behavioral (what you're doing) component. What about the obsessive thoughts that don't appear to involve the elaborate rituals that accompany forms of OCD you read about earlier in this book? What can you do to rein in those nagging thoughts?

The famous poet John Milton wrote, "The mind is its own place" (Milton 2003), and it doesn't take a lot of investigation to make out that he was pretty much right. The thoughts that swirl around in our heads are, to a great extent, beyond our control and represent an astounding range of ideas, internal chatter, memories, and vivid images of near and far-off futures. The mind's amazing capacity for creative imagery of the past, present, and future may include some pretty scary stuff—the stuff that writers, artists, and composers of great mystery novels, horror and suspense movies, and eerie paintings and music know well. Most of the time, we can dismiss our most distressing imagery of scary things that could happen to either ourselves or our loved ones. It doesn't seem to affect our day-to-day functioning all that much. But what happens when this stuff replays over and over in our heads like a broken record?

Many mental disorders are characterized by recurrent bad thoughts, including major depression, post-traumatic stress disorder (PTSD), and generalized anxiety disorder. In the following pages, we'll discuss the form of OCD that is characterized by bad thoughts.

Primarily Obsessional OCD

One of the most distressing and challenging forms of OCD is the type characterized by persistent unwanted and intrusive thoughts that are not specifically associated with compulsive rituals—a form known as *primarily obsessional OCD*. If you struggle with this variety of OCD, distressing and unwanted thoughts pop into your head frequently. These thoughts typically center on a fear that you will lose conscious control of yourself or your faculties, that you may do something totally uncharacteristic of yourself, something ghastly and harmful— potentially fatal, even—to yourself or others. You may have vivid images of these acts and even feel real impulses to commit them—although you will never actually succumb to these impulses. Your obsessive thoughts, quite likely, are of an aggressive or sexual nature, and probably elicit feelings of enormous guilt, shame, and embarrassment.

Examples of such intrusive thoughts include:

"What if I lose control of myself and stab my mother with a knife?"

"What if I inappropriately touch my baby's genital area?"

"What if I get an erection when looking at someone of the same sex?"

"What if I assault my teacher with a sharp pencil?"

"What if I poke my friend in the eye with a pick?"

"What if I lose control and shout a racial epithet?"

"What if I steal money without knowing it?"

"What if I burn my cat with a lit cigarette?"

"What if I lose control and harm myself?"

"What if I dump scalding water on my baby?"

"What if I think a bad thought about God?"

"What if I lose control of myself and go crazy?"

"What if I drive my car into oncoming traffic?"

"What if I'm not really gay?"

Common to all of these diverse thoughts is this underlying theme: "What if I were to snap, lose control of myself, and do something totally uncharacteristic of me—perhaps even without my knowing it—that results in harm to myself or someone else?" The anxiety accompanying these ideas is typically very intense, and you may experience heart palpitations and sweating when they come up. You may form mental associations with the situations in which the thoughts occurred and try to avoid similar situations in the future—at all costs!

In the past, this form of OCD was referred to as *obsessions without compulsions* or *pure obsessions* because psychologists observed that many people had such thoughts without such obvious compulsive behaviors as washing or checking. But more recent studies of obsessive thoughts (Salkovskis et al. 1999 and Freeston et al. 1997) present rather strong evidence that "purely" obsessive thoughts are, in fact, accompanied by subtle compulsive habits, in the form of such mental rituals as *thought recall*, the conscious remembering of the past to reassure oneself that the horrific act didn't happen; self-reassurance seeking called *testing*; and avoidance of thought through a process known as *thought suppression*. Now this is pretty subtle, technical stuff, but the least you need to know is that because of these discoveries, most psychologists have replaced the old term, "pure obsession," with the current handle for this variety, "primarily obsessional OCD."

Does This Sound Familiar?

As mentioned earlier, only a clinical expert can correctly diagnose any variety of OCD. But there is a vast amount of clinical observation and research that points to very consistent patterns of thought and behavior among people struggling with primarily obsessional OCD. If many of the following sound familiar, you may be wrestling with this challenging condition:

- Your obsessive thoughts depict you in a manner that is the *total opposite* of your actual behavior, previous history, or personality. Your intrusive thoughts are wholly uncharacteristic of who you are.

- Though you experience these thoughts, feelings, and impulses as extremely vivid, intense, and frightening, you never act upon these thoughts—ever!

- You spend a great deal of time worrying, "What if I'm misdiagnosed and don't have OCD but some other god-awful mental illness?"

- Not only do you feel extreme guilt about having these thoughts—for example, worrying that you are a bad parent, partner, or person—but you also worry a great deal about the horrific consequences if you were to "snap" and act upon your thoughts. You frequently fear being arrested or charged with child abuse, having your children taken away, or being damned to hell.

- Your obsessive thoughts cause you an enormous sense of guilt and shame. The operational idea is, "If I think it, it must mean that I secretly wish to do it. Therefore, I'm an awful, disgusting, horrible person at heart, and I should probably be punished or isolated from society for having such bad thoughts. I also should protect others from my potentially evil actions."

- You tend to place excessive emphasis on over-controlling your thoughts, feelings, and behaviors.

Unsurprisingly, primarily obsessional OCD can have very significant effects on your social life. Primarily obsessional OCD is perhaps the least understood form of OCD, and is certainly among the most misunderstood of all psychiatric disorders. Consequently, you probably find your experience of these thoughts both puzzling and frightening.

You may have sought to hide your obsessive thoughts from your most trusted and beloved friends, family members, and even from mental health professionals you've consulted. If you don't get treatment for your obsessive thoughts, you may make life-altering decisions regarding your "fitness" for marriage, parenthood, or a career based on them. Untreated, this form of OCD can surely rob you of your future.

Episodes of primarily obsessional OCD usually occur during periods of high stress, such as the loss of a loved one, marital problems, or career setbacks. But they may be aggravated even by positive major life transitions and achievements, such as getting married, having your first child, advancing in your career, moving to a new locale, retiring, finding yourself in an "empty nest" after your children have left home, and so forth. Also note, this form of OCD is frequently associated with both pre- and postpartum psychological distress.

Why Am I Having These Thoughts?

While the exact cause of primarily obsessional OCD is unknown, some OCD researchers have observed that particular brain structures that regulate our thoughts and emotions, such as the caudate nucleus, may be impaired in people with OCD (Baxter et al. 1992). Their brains may not do such a good job of regulating what thoughts come into their awareness, leading them to focus on certain abstract possibilities that most people would dismiss unconsciously. As with other forms of OCD, levels of the brain chemical serotonin may also be imbalanced in people with primarily obsessional OCD, and it is well established that medications for enhancing serotonin in the brain do help reduce the intensity and frequency of intrusive thoughts in many individuals with this form of the disorder. Genetics may also play a role in whether you experience this particular variety of OCD.

From a psychological perspective, there exists evidence (Rachman and de Silva 1978) that your obsessive thoughts are, in fact, no different from the disturbing and disruptive thoughts of people who do not have OCD. The big difference is that, if you have OCD, instead of just passing through your mind like a train going by a station, these thoughts seem to get stuck in your head, replaying over and over again.

One of the psychological factors that seems to play a role in this state of "stuckness" is called *thought/action fusion*. This is the tendency of people with OCD to place a great deal of importance on the meaning and content of their thoughts, equating the thoughts with the horrific deeds they refer to. If you have this symptom, you experience the *thought* of doing something horrific to yourself or someone else as equivalent to actually *doing* it. You interpret your own bad thoughts as omens of bad things that either have happened in the past or will happen in the future. If you have these kinds of obsessive thoughts, you might experience great guilt just because you thought about plowing your car into a crowded bus shelter as you harmlessly drove by. Since your thoughts are instant and virtually infinite in scope, and come as naturally to you as blinking your eyes, the potential for suffering is especially great when you're struggling with primarily obsessional OCD.

Am I Going Crazy?

It sounds like too much to bear! You may wonder whether, at some point, you'll become so anxious, so frightened, so desperately engulfed in this trap that you'll actually snap—that you'll lose control and do the very horrific things you fear most. Fortunately, the answer is a simple no. And the reason is, no matter how much anxiety you feel or how horrific are the ideas buzzing around in your head, your core personality—the person you and others know you to be, your basic instincts, moral fiber, and sense of right and wrong—remains well intact even through your worst OCD nightmare. Your OCD is your OCD—it's not you!

Another fact about OCD is that, while the disorder can occur alongside any other mental disorder, including psychotic disorders, the intrusive thoughts of someone with OCD have little or nothing in common with the psychotic thoughts of people with disorders such as schizophrenia. Many primarily obsessionals have been shaken by news stories splashed all over the media of seemingly normal mothers and fathers suddenly losing control and drowning or otherwise harming their own children. When the details of these stories are finally revealed, what becomes clear is that the parents suffered from delusions caused by a psychiatric illness or condition, such as paranoid schizophrenia or antisocial personality disorder, which have nothing in common with OCD.

How Do I Know for Sure?

If you experience primarily obsessional OCD, it's common for you to doubt whether you really have OCD at all. After all, you may spend a good deal of your time worrying whether you'll chop up your coworkers or whisk the neighbor's baby off to the toolshed. You may wonder whether you actually have one of those other psychiatric illnesses we mentioned that do sometimes incline people to carry out horrible and tragic acts. As a result of this doubt, you may spend a great deal of time on the Internet seeking out websites on such subjects as pedophilia, aggression, self-injury, being gay and the process of "coming out," psychosis, various sexual deviances, and so forth. You may do this with the intention of making "absolutely certain" that you are not a pedophile or sexual deviant, a potential serial killer or ax murderer, or whatnot.

Beware that the result of this endeavor is *always* the same: the relief you anticipate from your research never happens. In much the same way that your attempts to avoid thinking about something continually refresh and re-evoke it in your mind, your fact-finding missions into the depths of abnormal human behavior only deepen the grip of the OCD by intensifying the doubt, increasing intrusive thoughts and anxiety, and encouraging and strengthening any compulsive measures you use to rid yourself of the doubts. Besides, it wastes a whole lot of time!

Fortunately, there is one way you can evaluate whether you merely have obsessive thoughts or are in the grip of some criminal madness. Consider for a moment the common obsessive thought of people who suffer from this variety of OCD: "What if I'm really a pedophile, lose control of myself, and assault a child?" If you take a hard look at the differences between a true pedophile and someone with OCD, some very significant differences are apparent.

True pedophiles derive great pleasure from their abusive actions. They actively seek out opportunities for this form of gratification and feel little guilt or remorse over their acts, at least until they're caught. They usually have some previous history of predatory sexual behavior toward others, and worry little about the consequences of their abusive behavior.

On the other hand, someone with primarily obsessional OCD who worries that he or she might be a pedophile feels utter shock and horror at the very idea of having such a thought. This person actively avoids situations in which such thoughts are likely to occur, or endures those situations with great difficulty. This person feels significant guilt over having the thoughts; worries about the consequences of acting upon them (such as going to jail, losing custody of the children, and being abandoned by family members); and typically has no previous history of sexual predatory behavior.

Not very similar, are they? The bottom line is that people with OCD, in fact, are extremely different from the people they often fear themselves to be. Unfortunately, when you're experiencing such horrific thoughts and the accompanying frightening emotions, it's extremely difficult, if not impossible, to clearly discern the facts of your situation. The anxiety-driven quest for certainty and reassurance skews every thought and only feeds the vicious cycle. A vast amount of clinical experience with OCD patients confirms this essential fact: If you were the person depicted by these thoughts, you would not be in such distress about them.

Mental Compulsions

Psychologists recognize at least three distinct behaviors that can be considered subtle mental compulsions, which help fuel the cycle of obsessive thoughts.

Thought Suppression

As briefly mentioned earlier in this chapter, one mental compulsion is a form of compulsive avoidance behavior called *thought suppression*. This is either a conscious or unconscious attempt to avoid thinking disturbing thoughts, to do everything possible to keep the thoughts from occurring. This compulsion tends to be very common in people who place a great deal of importance on personally controlling their thoughts, feelings, and behaviors. There are different ways of understanding the cognitive mechanism of thought suppression, but there is some consensus that attempting to over-control and eradicate thoughts serves only to energize and generate the very thoughts one is trying to avoid. There is ample evidence (Wegner 1994) that it is these very attempts to avoid, suppress, or otherwise prevent these thoughts from occurring that contributes to their frequency and intensity in people with primarily obsessional OCD.

You can test out this idea on yourself by doing a little experiment: Get comfortable in your chair or wherever you happen to be. If it's convenient, switch off any distractions and maybe dim the lights. Now take about a minute and conjure in your mind the image of an empty cobalt-blue glass bottle, the kind you might have seen from time to time in an import store or antique shop. The light that passes through the bottle seems an impossibly deep blue. Maybe the bottle is old and bears the marks of time, such as a chip here and there, or scratches on the base or at the lip. Roll the bottle around in your mind, seeing it from each side. If there is a breeze, maybe you can hear its faint, hollow whistle as it passes over the bottle's neck. Really concentrate on the image of this bottle. Spend about a minute or so imagining that bottle in as much detail as possible.

Now, set this book down on your lap. For the next two minutes, give yourself this single task: Don't think about the blue bottle. Think about anything you want, but no matter what, don't think about the bottle. Go ahead. We'll wait for you.

Well, how did you do? Did you make it a full two minutes without that bottle flashing through your mind? While it's not impossible, it was probably pretty hard for you to keep from thinking about the bottle.

Now, instead of trying to avoid something as neutral as a blue glass bottle, imagine that the thought was of taking this bottle and whacking it over the head of your best friend, beloved sibling, or coworker, literally bludgeoning and bloodying them—something you'd normally never imagine doing in a million years! You think, "Does that make me bad? Does that mean I'm going to lose control?" For a person with OCD, the doubts and worries begin to swirl to the point at which it seems like a matter of greatest importance to be sure *not* to think those very thoughts! But the more you try to avoid the thought, the more prevalent in your mind it becomes. If you place a premium on controlling your thoughts, the less control over them you will have, as well as the more anxiety, ultimately resulting in even more anxiety, more thoughts, more suppression, and so on. Eventually you'll find yourself engulfed in a vicious cycle of ever-intensifying bad thoughts and elaborate measures to control them.

Avoidance is the central means by which primarily obsessional OCD sufferers control their discomfort and anxiety. If you engage in avoidance in addition to using thought suppression, you may also avoid people, things, and situations that trigger these thoughts. This can include avoiding social gatherings, public places, young children, pets, sharp objects, and necessary child-care tasks such as diapering your baby or bathing your young children. If you must partake in these situations, you probably do so reluctantly, enduring them with a great deal of discomfort.

Compulsive Certainty Seeking

Another mental compulsion is called *compulsive certainty seeking*. If you suffer from primarily obsessional OCD, you probably have a very low tolerance for uncertainty. When a situation arises that doesn't afford you absolute certainty that you won't act upon your bad thoughts, you will invariably experience extreme anxiety and try to engage in some certainty-seeking behavior to contain that anxiety. This often takes the form of mentally reviewing the recent or remote past for reassurance that you are not as depicted in your intrusive thought. You may start anxiously reviewing over and over in your mind whether that innocent light touch on the arm of your six-year-old nephew during family dinner last night was really an inappropriate attempt to grope his privates. Or you may wonder whether that paper clip from the office that you discovered when you arrived home had accidentally fallen into your purse constitutes stealing from your place of employment. Eventually, you may find yourself spending a great deal of time and energy combing through your storehouse of recent and remote memories, desperately trying to reassure yourself that no misdeed occurred.

When you involve others in your certainty seeking, the behavior is known as *reassurance seeking*, a very common behavior seen in primarily obsessional OCD sufferers. Reassurance seeking takes the form of an anxious request to others, most often a family member or authority, such as a mental health professional, to confirm that some inappropriate behavior did not take place. If you engage in reassurance requesting, although you otherwise may be fully in control of your senses and faculties, you decide that you cannot trust your senses or memory of events occurring even minutes ago.

Often your requests for reassurance are repetitive. You may often expect them to be complied with in a particular manner, with a certain tone of voice or volume, and without distraction. When your requirements are not met, you may repeat your request over and over. Loved ones of people with primarily obsessional OCD often report how maddening and painful this particular compulsion is for them to experience. If you engage in this behavior, you probably know how painful other people's reactions can be when you ask them again and again to dispel your doubts. Because of this common negative reaction, you might turn to inanimate sources of reassurance such as books or the Internet. But, as previously mentioned, searching on the Internet for information to reassure yourself that you are not in danger or dangerous is another form of compulsive certainty seeking that ultimately only inflames your intrusive thoughts.

Testing

Testing is another compulsive certainty-seeking behavior very commonly employed by people with primarily obsessional OCD to relieve the anxiety of an obsessive thought. It is either a covert (hidden) or overt (easily seen) behavior that is persistent and repetitive, and may seem very odd to observers. There is a vast array of testing behaviors, depending on the content of the obsessive thought.

One example is a man who worries constantly that he might lose control of himself and sexually assault a child, whether his own or another. As a result of the severe anxiety this thought generates, he pays laserlike attention to "test" whether, in the presence of a child or some thing or situation evoking thoughts of a child, he experiences any feeling in his genitals, often going through elaborate and time-consuming mental rituals to determine for certain whether or not "it moved." Testing compulsions are intended to relieve the anxiety provoked by horrific thoughts, but often the anxiety is so great that it can generate "phantom" feelings and sensations in the body, feeding the relentless cycle of intrusive thoughts, anxiety, more doubting, and more testing.

Another example is a woman who thinks she could lose control and drive her car into oncoming traffic, killing herself and her family. Her response to this anxiety-provoking thought is to test the idea by sharply turning the wheel of her car while driving, to see whether she will follow through with the impulse dictated by her obsessive thought. She may do this three to five times while driving at high speed—to the sheer and utter horror of family members riding helplessly in the car. At the end of her test, this woman may feel satisfied that she won't lose control, and get momentary relief from the thought. But, of course, her obsession will return during the next driving episode. Over time this testing will become a repetitive and persistent habit that she cannot avoid performing. Although her job, family, and social life depend upon it, driving a car can become a daily nightmare for her.

All three of these mental compulsions—thought suppression, certainty seeking, and testing—are barriers to the kind of engagement with your intrusive thoughts that can bring about real relief from OCD. To make progress toward a well-lived life that isn't driven by your OCD, you'll need to learn how to disengage from obsessive thoughts without relying on mental rituals. Let's see how to do it.

Disengaging from Intrusive Thoughts

In this section, we'll take a look at some things you can do to help you let go of your struggle with those unwanted and disturbing thoughts. As mentioned at the beginning of this chapter, these techniques can be valuable to you whether you experience primarily obsessional OCD or another, more overtly ritualistic variety. Even though you have little control over the substance of your thoughts, we will show you that thoughts themselves need exert little control over what you do, how you feel, and what you accomplish. The upside to having little control over your thoughts is that, likewise, your thoughts have little control over you—unless you let them. The following techniques are basic strategies you can use to respond to your thoughts in ways that take power away from them and give it back to you.

Starting with Acceptance

Think about all of the things in your life that you can do absolutely nothing about. If your scheduled golf game got rained out, those are the breaks. No amount of wishing and carrying on will bring back that crosstown bus you just missed, now that it has pulled away from the curb and disappeared into rush-hour traffic. There's a lot you can do to have your life the way you want it, but then there's an awful lot that just happens and all you can do is watch it unfold. As little children, we had our own way of dealing with this less-than-satisfying aspect of life. We wailed, thrashed around, and pounded our tiny fists on the ground. But as we grew up, we internalized the bitter lesson that a big part of life involves accepting what is and just making the best of it.

Or, at least most of us learned that lesson—and abide by it most of the time. However, despite what we can acknowledge with our rational minds, we do keep wailing, thrashing, and pounding our fists against some of the facts of life, even well past childhood. If you're like many people wrestling with primarily obsessional OCD, you probably struggle against your distressing thoughts. "Why, oh why," you wonder, "am I like this? Why do I think these terrible things?"

A good way to start disengaging from disturbing, obsessive thoughts is to accept them whenever possible. We discussed acceptance in chapter 2, but it is especially relevant to the issue of obsessive thoughts. If you remember nothing else, remember that OCD is something you have, not something you are. You have OCD in the same way that you might have a cold, diabetes, thyroid disease, or asthma. But these are just qualities you possess. They don't define you. More and more, science points to the conclusion that your inclination to have obsessive thoughts is a neurobehavioral brain glitch, a "hiccup" in your mind. The hiccup results from a vicious cycle of habitual responses to fear-provoking mental content that inadvertently increases your pain as you desperately try to alleviate it. By learning that it's tolerable for you to have these thoughts, and by accepting them instead of battening down the hatches for a perfect storm of mental anguish, you'll amaze yourself with how much energy and strength you can summon to do good things in your life.

And, while you practice accepting your distressing thoughts, here's something else for you to think about: When you boil it down, the content of your distressing thoughts is not the problem; rather, what causes your pain and frustration is how you respond to the content of your thoughts. You've taken a lifetime to learn how to be tense, fearful, anxious, and angry in response to these thoughts. But that doesn't mean it has to be this way. If you choose, you can learn to respond differently to your thoughts, observing them and letting them slip back into the mental ooze from whence they came without engaging with them. This is where most therapy for OCD goes awry—in getting all caught up in the content and meaning of your thoughts instead of focusing on the process of how these intrusive and mostly irrelevant thoughts get stuck in the loop of your mind.

Changing Your Response to the Thoughts

If the problem of obsessive thoughts is not the thoughts themselves or their content but your response to them, then let's talk about some more-skillful responses that can actually short-circuit your OCD. Just as we mentioned in our discussion of thought suppression, at least part of the repetitive quality of obsessive thoughts is caused by the reinforcing verbal event you engage in when trying *not* to think them—remember the blue glass bottle? What if, instead of harboring an attitude of avoidance at any price (which only makes matters worse), you tried on an attitude of accepting the thought? This might be a radical notion for you, and we'll grant that it probably sounds scary as hell. But why not just try it?

We'll assume that you are reading this in, at least, relative comfort. Maybe you're at home in your room, feeling calm and more-or-less free from the things that might trigger and aggravate your OCD. In this quiet place, you have a good opportunity to get a feel for how this new attitude might affect you. Without trying to summon up your disturbing thoughts, take a moment and say or think one or more of the following with intention:

- "I'll just allow this thought to be there."

- "I will go about my day in full and complete acceptance of the 'glitchy' thoughts my OCD puts into my head."

- "I will allow my horrible thoughts to take up space in my mind for a while."

- "While I don't have to like this thought, I fully accept its being there."

How did it feel? Scary? Overwhelming? If it was a lot to take in, try it again. Repeat the intentions above until you can really sit with them, feeling what they mean for you and what kinds of reactions they evoke in your body. Especially pay attention to the sensations that you feel in your chest and the rate of your breathing. Do you feel dampness on your brow or in your palms? It's totally fine if you do. Just pay attention to it without judgment. If, after a while, you can hold these intentions in your mind, you can move on to the following even more radical declarations of acceptance.

- "I welcome these bad thoughts with an open mind."

- "Thank you, mind, for that horrifying thought."

- "I can think that thought—and a lot worse, too—without being harmed or harming others. These are just thoughts that I'm having. They have no power over me."

- "Come on, bad thought—come and stay awhile!"

As you rehearse these declarations, be vigilant for any sense you might have that they will either make your obsessive thoughts go away or lessen your anxiety in any way. They won't; they can't. And if you try to make them serve this function for you, you'll create new compulsions and trade one bad mental habit for another. Remember that it's axiomatic with OCD that *any mental or physical action performed in response to an obsessive thought that immediately reduces the anxiety of that obsession will automatically become another compulsion.* Compulsions serve to alleviate your anxiety. These affirmations, on the other hand, have the paradoxical purpose of bringing you closer to, and deeper into, your feelings of fear and anxiety, which is the one sure way of minimizing the power these feelings have to shape your life and take you in directions you don't want to go.

Mental Judo?

Have you ever heard people describe judo, or another martial art, as a way of using an attacker's energy against him or her? Well, since one of the authors is a trained martial artist, we don't want to oversimplify these rich and complex practices by telling you to deal with your thoughts as a judoka would deal with a punch or kick. However, it is true that there is sometimes great value in being passive, flexible, and nonreactive toward something forceful and distressing, when you would normally be resistant, rigid, and defensive.

Think about some of the news footage you may have seen of a landscape after a hurricane has passed through. Telephone poles, trees, bridge supports, and other rigid, powerful structures are uprooted and destroyed, scattered about by the force of the gale. But grasses, reeds, and other light, flexible things pop back into place, seemingly unfazed by the tempest. When you are assailed by a distressing thought, another technique you can use is to simply passively ride it out, letting it exhaust its energy without reacting to it and then letting it pass as quickly as it came. You'll find this more effective than summoning all of your strength to meet "fire with fire."

Again, in the comfort of your reading chair or wherever you happen to be, ponder the following metaphor for a while. Don't try to conjure up any distressing thoughts; they would only be a distraction now, and you'll have plenty of time to practice letting go in real time later. For now, just read and take in the following scene, closely observing how it affects your body.

> *You're at the beach, swimming in a calm ocean. For some time, the surf has been gentle, rolling around you and leaving you bobbing comfortably in the ebb and flow. But you notice, out at the break line, that an unusually large and menacing wave has formed and crashed onto itself. A big wall of water moves toward you at a terrific clip. As it approaches, your heart starts pounding. The crest of the wave is as tall as you are and could easily drag you under.*
>
> *Your first reaction is to clench your body really tightly as the wave hits you, digging your feet into the sand and trying to maintain your footing. But, because you've read the acceptance chapter of* Coping with OCD, *you quickly consider the fact that water is really, really heavy and even a small wave packs the force of a fast-moving car. All the*

struggling you could do wouldn't keep you upright
as this whitecap tears over you. So instead of fighting
it, you decide to calmly watch the wave come toward
you. As it approaches, you take a deep breath and
relax. Opening your arms and legs, you become
lighter on your feet. You literally embrace the wave.
Your open posture makes you slide up the front of the
swell, riding gently up over the wave. You soar over
the main body of water as it passes toward the shore.
Coming down the back side of the swell, you find
yourself unharmed and in more or less the same spot
where you were when you began. The wave fizzles
out on the sand. Gulls squawk overhead. The sun
sparkles on the water around you.

How did that feel? Can you see how this metaphor might be useful to you when you experience a bad thought? If you spend some time rehearsing the wave metaphor, you may find that you can call it to mind when confronted with an unwanted obsessive thought. When the thought comes up, allow it to pass by without resisting or fighting it. By watching the thought pass through instead of fighting it, you can learn to deepen your capacity for acceptance and tolerance of the thought.

If I Accept and Tolerate, Does That Make Me Bad?

No, no, no! The fact that you can accept the occurrence of a bad thought does not mean that you approve of its contents. Have you heard those disclaimer statements they always read on radio or TV networks after broadcasting a local op-ed piece? A townsperson gets on the air and vents his spleen about rising gas prices, suburban creep, or the overcommercialization of Christmas. And as soon as this person has said his piece, the husky-voiced announcer in the background returns and makes it clear that the views just expressed are solely those of the commentator, not the producers, the station, or the network. If only every obsessive thought came with a disclaimer like that! You could think about stuffing your hand in the paper shredder or pouring bleach in your spouse's coffee—and then a little voice would say, "The preceding horrible thought came out of nowhere and is in no way indicative of the character or moral fiber of the thinker."

All of us have bad thoughts that do not reflect who we are or what we are about. Remember what we said about having little control over our thoughts? Don't pay attention to the content of your obsessive thoughts; detach yourself from their meaning. You accept the thought because you have little choice if you want to free yourself from the suffering it normally brings you. But your acceptance does not endorse the content of the thought or accept it as fact. Remember that your decision to accept it actually drains the thought of its power and intensity.

Will I Lose Control by Accepting and Tolerating?

Some people consider their anxiety and worry about a distressing thought to be "insurance" against their acting on it. Worrying constantly that you might throw the cat into traffic or toss the hair dryer into your spouse's bathwater may reassure you that you won't actually commit these atrocities. But the acceptance strategies in this chapter may have rather dramatic power to reduce your anxiety—although, as we mentioned, they are not *intended* to do so! As your anxiety decreases, you may feel in great danger of losing control and acting on your obsessive thoughts. You may have an unwanted thought, even accept it, and then scan yourself for anxiety, revulsion, or disgust. When you don't find the usual negative feelings, you may head back to the Internet to look up the criteria for pedophilia or sociopathic behavior one more time.

Well, guess what? This is just another thought. As it says on the shampoo label, "Lather, rinse, repeat." If you start worrying that you're not appropriately horrified at yourself for thinking an intrusive thought, you've done something right. Apply your acceptance affirmations or the wave metaphor to your thoughts about worry, and keep at it until you really get the fact that your thoughts can pass through you without doing harm. Unlike the misleading instruction on the shampoo bottle to "repeat"—a ruse concocted by shampoo manufacturers to sell more products and give you split ends, which will send you off to buy more of their conditioners—repeatedly practicing an attitude of acceptance actually works.

ERP for Bad Thoughts

You'll remember from back in chapter 3 that ERP is an effective tool whose purpose is to bring about habituation, or "nervous system boredom," in anxiety-provoking situations. If your OCD is one of the more overt varieties—you wash, check, hoard, or whatnot—you may have already gone through the process of exposure described in the previous chapter. ERP can be used effectively for your thoughts, too. The process is a little different for obsessive thoughts, if only because it is a little hard to intentionally expose yourself to something that runs fleetingly through your brain from time to time. If you have contamination issues, you can go into the alley, touch the inside of a trash dumpster, and then touch all of the pristinely maintained surfaces in your home and make remarkable progress in a surprisingly short time span. Exposure to intrusive thoughts is trickier, but it is accomplished through the same *imaginal* and *in vivo* exposure methods we described back in chapter 3. Now let's take a look at how they are applied to the symptoms of primarily obsessive OCD.

Imagining the Worst

Imaginal exposure requires that you practice holding in your mind the most vivid, horrific image you can endure that is associated with your particular obsessive thought. By repeatedly holding this image without attempting to suppress or neutralize its discomfort several minutes per day for one to three weeks in a row, the thought will begin to lose its impact and control over you.

To assist you in conjuring this image, write it down in the form of a brief, three- to five-minute narrative. Write it down in first person, a little story of your "worst nightmare." Here are some things to be sure to include:

- The situation that triggers the thought

- Your decision whether to act upon this horrific thought

- The moment you lose control over yourself

- The devastating emotions you experience

- What this says about you as a person

- The terrible consequences you experience as a result of your misdeed

Below is an example. Of course, your narrative will be determined by the particular thoughts you struggle with.

I'm in the kitchen making vegetable soup. My two-year-old sits across the room in her high chair, mashing peas into a paste on the tray. The thought occurs to me that there is every reason to suspect that, while turning a carrot, I will feel the need to send the chef's knife careering across the room, plunging into my child's eye. In a moment of weakness, I give in to this impulse. I see one of her big, blue eyes gaping at me like a round, watery bull's-eye. I take the knife by the back of the blade like a carnival performer and, despite the gut-wrenching horror I feel in the process, fling the blade through the air. Helpless to divert it from its terrible course, I watch it slice through empty space like an arrow. All the while, my child coos at me, innocent of the danger she faces. There is a subtle shift in

her expression a split second before the knifepoint
plunges into her eye, a knowing look of fear, pain,
and vulnerability. I'm crushed. It was bad enough
that I was so careless as to make soup with a helpless
toddler in the kitchen. That I succumbed to the
desire to disfigure and probably slaughter my child
makes me the vilest sort of monster, an infanticidal
maniac. I don't deserve to live. Although I call for
help right away, it's too late. My child is pinned to
the high chair like a moth in a glass case, her life
draining away as I weep over her. The police come
and drag me to jail. At the trial, my wife, who has
since divorced me and refuses to take my calls, begs
the judge to hand down the severest sentence the law
permits. He decides that lethal injection is too good
for me. Instead, he remands me to a solitary wing
of a forgotten prison, where I rot the rest of my life
away in misery, self-recrimination, and remorse.

Just writing your narrative on paper will probably initially trigger a high level of anxiety and discomfort. This is exactly what you need to happen, so just sit with the anxiety. Let it come over you as it will, and then let it pass on its own. You can revisit your written narrative by rereading it or recording it onto a cassette tape, CD, or DVD. Read it with a clear voice, expressively and even somewhat dramatically. Read or listen to your narrative over and over, starting with short sessions and working up to an hour or more. If you make a recording, listen to it as often as possible. Play it in your car or put it on in the background while you're doing housework (although you may want to be sure that no one is listening who might misunderstand your intentions). Go ahead and immerse yourself in this scary stuff without holding back. It's cathartic and helpful to experience this anxiety full force. It may be uncomfortable, but it's certainly not dangerous. You may want to make note of your SUDS level after every few repetitions of the narrative, just to keep track of your progress.

If you are a visual learner with an artistic bent, you might draw your narrative. Use large sheets of paper and colored pens, pencils, or markers. Each drawing should depict another scene in the evolving nightmare. It doesn't actually matter whether or not you are a talented artist. You can easily render the characters in your nightmare using stick figures and simple lines. Make a few copies of the same narrative drawings, and place them in obvious places within your normal everyday environment for easy viewing. Notice how your anxiety goes up and down throughout the exposure experience.

The goal is not to reduce your anxiety down to zero all at once; reducing it a little each day is fine. It's more important to endure the discomfort for as long as possible while noticing how your *thoughts about the thoughts* begin to change. Your thoughts about the thoughts, what they mean, and their impact upon you will probably become far less reactive and catastrophic, and much more objective. The ultimate goal of the exercise is to help you realize that a thought is just a thought. This may take days, weeks, or months to accomplish, but it's certainly within your grasp. If you find this exercise too harrowing to fully complete, do it in stages. But pay attention to the natural tendency to avoid the discomfort of exposure to these thoughts. You can only reach your goal of increased behavioral flexibility if you allow yourself to feel the pain of your obsessive thoughts.

Combining Imaginal and In Vivo Exposure

In vivo exposure, or confronting one's intrusive and fear-provoking thoughts in the actual, real-life situations in which they occur, can be combined with imaginal exposure to maximize progress in managing intrusive obsessions. For example, if your imaginal exposure narrative was similar to the sample passage, involving the idea of stabbing someone you care about with a knife, you might combine your narrative with the in vivo experience of actually holding a knife in the presence of your loved one. If your narrative dealt with the fear that you might touch a child inappropriately, your in vivo exposure might involve changing a baby's diaper while listening through headphones to an exposure narrative that describes your touching a child in the "wrong way." This combination of imaginal and in vivo exposures will create a very strong initial rush of discomfort, but with time and repetition, you'll habituate to the point of realizing that, no matter how strong your thoughts or how seemingly vulnerable and "risky" the situation, a thought is still just a thought. Because you are who you are (and even with OCD, you are always you), you'll never—and we mean never—act on the contents of your obsessive thoughts.

In vivo exposure can be introduced in combination with imaginal exposure in a gradual, stepwise fashion. For example, while listening to your imaginal exposure narrative about stabbing someone with a knife, you can first place the knife several feet from you. Then, after habituating to that situation, move the knife closer and then still closer in successive exposures conducted on a daily basis for one to three weeks. Eventually you will be able to hold the knife in your hand while listening to your narrative. Again, you may well consider this situation too difficult to manage without professional help, and that is perfectly okay. But don't let that fear lead you to totally avoid the work. Instead, seek qualified professional help to guide you through this important exposure work.

Managing Intrusive Thoughts on the Fly

Some intrusive thoughts occur out of the blue and persist to some degree even after you've completed formal exposure work. You'll learn a lot more about this kind of thing in chapter 7, where we'll discuss lapses and relapses. But all you need to know for now is that you should expect obsessive thoughts to pop up from time to time, even when you've worked diligently on acceptance and ERP. Your best defense against this sort of thing is to develop a set of strategies to manage intrusive thoughts in flight, as they occur. No one strategy works for everybody, so you'll need to find the one that works best for you. Remember, the best strategy for managing OCD is not the one that immediately relieves your anxiety. In fact, that one will soon become just another compulsion and wind up refueling your OCD. Rather, the best strategy is the one that empowers you to withstand and remain resilient in the face of your compulsive urges until they recede on their own. These strategies work to put your OCD back on its heels, decreasing the amount of time you feel compelled to engage in compulsions. Here are some of the best strategies that have worked for the countless people who have gone bravely before you.

Magnifying

At the moment the intrusive thought occurs, vividly picture mentally the image of what that thought would look like if taken to the most extreme degree possible. Once you've done this, intensify the image with a provocative self-statement that borders on the absurd. For example, if you happen to feel some resonance with the kitchen narrative, you might use the thought, "What if I lose control and harm my child with a knife?" When the thought comes up, hold vividly in your mind the terrifying image of yourself snatching the knife from the counter and charging at your child while crying, "I'm going to cut you, and I'm going to like it!" If your intrusive thought has to do with your potentially sexually assaulting a child, picture yourself becoming inflamed with lust and losing control, and say to yourself, "Hot damn! I just can't wait to have a little fun with that child. This is the best thing that's happened to me in weeks!" It may be shocking at first, but the absurd excess of this approach, robustly embracing your worst nightmare, will actually suck the wind right out of your OCD, breaking its force and intensity. Many people in your situation find that magnification works very well in the moment a thought occurs, rapidly reducing the amount of time they feel stuck carrying out compulsions.

Watching and Waiting

If you have a keen imagination, you may find that magnification is your favorite coping strategy when distressing thoughts catch you unawares. But doing absolutely nothing in response to an intrusive thought might just be the most powerful tool you can use to deal with these painful and disturbing pop-ins. Doing nothing deprives your OCD of its tendency to latch onto a behavior that reduces the anxiety, simultaneously promoting the correct attitude of acceptance in the presence of the bad thought. Merely watching the thought, without judging it or insisting that it go away, gives it the opportunity to become extinct on its own. The simple act of doing nothing while remaining present and aware of your thought is tremendously powerful (as we'll discuss in greater detail in chapter 5). It reinforces the idea that you are merely the context in which OCD takes place, rather than an active agent of the disorder. Disturbing thoughts arising and falling away without your doing anything should clue you in to the fact that you can always choose to just give up the struggle with OCD

Refocusing

This response (courtesy of Dr. Jeffrey Schwartz, from his book *Brain Lock*) takes the "watch and wait" method a step further. At the moment you permit the thought to remain in your mind, gently shift to a new behavior that reflects your values and intentions, *as if you did not have the thought at all*. The idea here is *not* to avoid the discomfort but to distract yourself from your impulse to "do something" to reduce the anxiety. For example, if the thought, "What if I stab my child?" occurs as you stand in the kitchen cutting vegetables with a sharp knife, watch and wait through the discomfort of the thought by doing nothing different. Continue to slice and dice the vegetables (no avoidances!) and then *refocus* on another activity or behavior, such as conversing with your child, reaching for another veggie to slice, singing a song, noticing your breathing, or thinking of your favorite recipe or the pleasant events of the previous day. You may shift your focus many times as you wait out the storm. What matters most is that you are not deterred from living your life because of a bad thought.

Accepting Uncertainty

Since intrusive thoughts trigger certainty-seeking behaviors, an effective counterresponse on the fly is to simply surrender to the uncertainty at the moment the bad thought occurs. By saying to yourself, "If I am a knife-wielding terror (or a child molester or a violent serial killer), then I just am," or maybe, "I might be a danger to myself or others, or I might not be. I'll probably only know for sure one way or another once I do something, and I'll just have to cross that bridge when I come to it." This approach involves an active willingness to surrender to the uncertainty regarding the outcome of allowing your distressing thought to just be. This approach will raise your anxiety in the short run, but with practice over time, the discomfort will decrease.

Avoiding Avoidance

At this point you've doubtlessly got the idea that anything you do to avoid anxiety and distress is going to backfire on you and reinforce your tendency to feel anxious and distressed. The simple fact of the matter is that you're going to encounter situations in your everyday life that will trigger obsessive thoughts. You can use these situations as opportunities for growth by making a point of not avoiding them. Instead, use the tools described here to manage the thoughts and test your resolve to embrace rather than run from your fears. When you find a comfortable space where you can live without too much distress, find another uncomfortable situation. Keep trying to discover your limits and, with the techniques you've just read about, find ways to break through them. Like someone trying to build a strong body through weight lifting, you must encounter the resistance repeatedly to develop the strength to overcome it.

All of the above strategies are the tools in your toolbox, to be employed at any time to more effectively manage intrusive thoughts. The ideas in this chapter may appear radically different from how you've been trying to control your thoughts. But it is this new way of thinking about your thoughts that's the key to breaking free from the grip of OCD. Indeed, our willingness to give up the need to control our thoughts ultimately allows us to gain control over them.

Being Here Now (Even with OCD)

We've discussed previously that some kind of fear underlies all manifestations of OCD. If you have contamination issues, you fear getting sick or poisoned from something you came into contact with. Or you fear passing along the ill effects of contamination to others. If you have a checking compulsion, you fear the consequences of your negligence should you forget to lock the door, turn off the stove, and so on. If you struggle with obsessive thoughts, there are any number of scenarios you may fear: inappropriately touching a child, causing the death of your mother-in-law with your bad thoughts, driving your car into oncoming traffic, and so forth. The list goes on.

But here is a question for you: what's the one thing that's common to all of these fears (besides that they're all related to

OCD)? In form, these fears are all very diverse. The chances are slim that anyone would experience all of them at once. Some of these fears pop up at home; others grip you in public. You may wrestle with some fears alone, while other ones may be prompted by contact with another person. When you examine these various fears, they don't seem to have much to do with one another. But if you look closely, they all have at least one very significant detail in common: all of the fears associated with OCD are alike in that they focus on misfortunes that may occur at some point in time other than *now*.

It is pretty ridiculous to even try to imagine OCD-related fears that focus on events happening in the present moment. If your car suddenly careers off the street into a crowded sidewalk café, you haven't the slightest cause to worry *whether* you will lose control of it. If your house is in flames around you, you won't give a second thought to the stove or its knobs. If you're running a high fever and your skin is turning red, the last thing on your mind is whether you could catch something from a doorknob or public toilet. None of this matters since OCD thoughts focus on what might happen in the future or has occurred in the past. It's true that many people with OCD think the rituals they perform now will somehow positively affect the future, but it's pretty obvious what the real object of that thought is: the *consequence* of doing or not doing something now, which can only exist in the future.

Another way to look at this is to regard the past and future as the "natural habitat" of OCD. Like a fish on dry land, in the present moment OCD doesn't have the conditions it needs to survive—uncertainty about the state of affairs in either the past or the future. Without these, OCD may flop around for a while with a glassy and surprised look in its eye, but eventually it will gasp its last breath and wither away.

Removing OCD from Its Natural Habitat

If you take a moment to really think about it, you'll probably realize that *all* of the distress you ever experienced from your OCD was related to calamities that *never* occurred when you felt anxious or ill at ease about them. In most cases, these misfortunes probably never occurred at all, but we're sure that they never happened during your distress over them.

If you've had a long history of struggling with OCD, this means that you've spent a good deal of your life living in a time other than the present. But you'll probably agree, at least intellectually, that the real business of living can only take place in that flying window of opportunity that we call "now." Every moment, "now" is slipping into the unchangeable past. At the same time, the unknowable future is getting its chance at being now. But just as quickly, it too slips into the past.

The unfunny joke of the situation is that you really don't get to pick when you want to live—it's now or never. We sometimes say that certain people "live in the past" or "live for the future," but this is really a language game, a play on words. We really mean that they're not *paying attention* to now, that they're focusing their attention on the past or the future. All the while, they're missing out on the one moment in time that is rich with vibrant life and possibilities—right now!

One of the most effective ways for you to move ahead in your new life, free from OCD, is to work on living in an environment where OCD can no longer subsist—the present moment. You can do this by learning to pay attention to your experiences as they happen—which is to say, you engage in a practice called *mindfulness*.

Not Just for Buddhists Anymore

Although much of the language used to describe it and many of the techniques used to foster it come from the Buddhist tradition, mindfulness is not a religious practice. It's simply one of many ways you can choose to experience the world. It just so happens that this particular way has been recognized for thousands of years, by a whole range of cultures, for the benefits it offers those who choose it: clarity of vision, compassion, thoughtfulness, and peace of mind. Because of these benefits, expressions of mindfulness are found in the contemplative traditions of many of the world's religions, including Christianity, Judaism, Islam, Hinduism, and others. But there is nothing at all religious, supernatural, or otherworldly in mindfulness. Quite the contrary, it is about being fully and intentionally connected to the very earthly here and now.

Noted psychologist and author Jon Kabat-Zinn famously defined mindfulness as "the awareness that emerges through paying attention on purpose, in the present moment and nonjudgmentally, to the unfolding of experience moment by moment" (Kabat-Zinn 2003). Perhaps more than any other figure, Kabat-Zinn has promoted a secular understanding of the idea of mindfulness. His research led to the development of *mindfulness-based stress reduction* (MBSR) in the 1980s, a technique that used mindfulness to assist people struggling with pain, illness, and stress. Since then, researchers have studied the effects of moment-to-moment awareness on the brain, and Dr. Hyman has repeatedly observed that the practice yields beneficial results. Many psychologists today are incorporating mindfulness practice into their client work. The practice is an important component of the so-called "third wave" behavior therapies such as *acceptance and commitment therapy* (ACT) and *dialectical behavior therapy* (DBT). With ever more attention being paid to it in the popular press, it's quite likely that mindfulness will soon be familiar to a great majority of Americans.

Starting a Journey with a Single Step

It's actually somewhat disingenuous for us to tell you that mindfulness is "good for OCD." It is—which is to say that a regular mindfulness practice may moderate your symptoms, help you through moments of anxiety, and decrease the frequency with which OCD "takes over" your life. But it's actually closer to the truth to tell you that mindfulness is good for you—period. All of the evidence available to us, both from research and the anecdotal reports of people who do mindfulness work, suggests that careful attention to each moment pays off in many areas of life. Relationships may deepen and become more intimate; anger may subside and be replaced by compassion and concern; depression may lift and be replaced by optimism and joy. Mindfulness can also help you separate your experience of events from your evaluations of and judgments *about* them, which is a very important distinction to make when you're wrestling with OCD.

Sounds pretty good, doesn't it? Well, of course there's a catch. Being mindful is not the easiest thing in the world to do. If you have any doubt about this, you can clear it up just by looking at your experience with OCD. How much time have you spent dwelling on the future or the past? One of the quirks of the human mind is that it can conjure memories or imagine possibilities that can be as absorbing and painful as actual events. We have the remarkable ability to actually do one thing while emotionally experiencing entirely another: Your body can stand alone in the shower while your mind argues with a coworker, sits across the desk from an IRS auditor, or bickers with your parents who live three states away.

Despite our tendencies to float off into the past or future, it is quite possible to train ourselves to live in the present moment. It's a long journey, and as these things generally do, it begins with a single step. Make your first mindfulness practices short and manageable, and try to set aside some time for them each day. As you progress in your work—when you can spend longer periods focusing closely on the present moment—you can increase the duration and scope of your practice. The good news is that, unlike ERP work, you'll probably enjoy the time you spend on mindfulness. You may even come to look forward to your practice periods as little vacations scattered throughout your day.

The mindfulness work you do during your practice periods, which some mindfulness practitioners would call "formal practice," is really training for being mindful throughout your day, a discipline known as "informal mindfulness" or "informal practice." Of course, it is much harder to be mindful in the middle of a crowded shopping mall or on a rumbling streetcar than in a silent corner of your house, when you're sitting in a comfortable chair. But by practicing mindfulness formally, you start to learn what it feels like to be mindful at all. Over time, you can train yourself to remain mindful, even when you have to attend to other distractions.

Informal mindfulness can help you with OCD in a couple of ways. Not only can it help you catch your anxious, OCD-related thoughts "in flight" and let them pass without getting too worked up about them, but it can also help you observe distressing objects or situations closely without reacting to them. In other words, mindfulness can paradoxically help you get distance from your OCD while bringing it closer to you so that you can learn to accept and experience it without letting it take over your life. In this second way, mindfulness work can really assist you in getting the most out of ERP by helping you engage with distressing situations without responding to them.

What follows in this chapter is just the barest, toe-in-the-water introduction to mindfulness practice and how you can apply its techniques to your day-to-day OCD experience. If you find this work helpful—and we think you will—we strongly recommend that you read some books that specifically spell out how to build a regular mindfulness practice. We particularly like *Calming Your Anxious Mind*, by Dr. Jeffrey Brantley (2007), but others are described in chapter 8.

Exercise: Just a Minute!

Your first mindfulness exercise is more of a self-test than the basis of a regular practice. It's a drill that is commonly taught

to beginners because it powerfully demonstrates how disconnected we can be from the actual passing of time. If you find
that you often feel hurried, you may sense the passing of time
as occurring more quickly than it's really moving. On the other
hand, if your perception of time runs too slowly, you may often
find yourself late for appointments and other obligations. This
exercise will give you a good idea of whether your internal clock
runs too fast or slow. It will also show you what it feels like to be
very attentive and focused for just one minute, which, repeated
over and over again, is all a mindfulness practice really is.

- Sit comfortably in a chair or on a cushion in a quiet
  part of your home or in some peaceful setting when
  you won't likely be disturbed.

- Loosen your collar and your belt. Get comfortable.
  If you're wearing a watch, take it off, but keep it
  close at hand.

- Take a few deep breaths. Once you do, take a look
  at your watch. As its sweep hand passes twelve, set
  your watch aside or turn it over in your hand so that
  you can't see its face.

- Now just sit comfortably and breathe normally until
  you sense that one minute has elapsed. (Oh, and don't
  cheat by counting the seconds. It may be tempting,
  but it defeats the purpose of the exercise.)

- Check your watch and note how much time has
  passed.

How did it go? Do you feel that you have a good sense of time, or were you surprised by how long or short your minute actually was? Remember that your purpose here is to develop an intentional and attentive relationship with the present moment, and an accurate perception of the passing of time is a good place to start. Think about what the results of this exercise might mean for you. Also, you may want to make a note of where your thoughts wandered while you were waiting for the minute to go by. Did the Doomsayer show up to tell you that something was amiss? If you took well more than a minute to complete this exercise and OCD-related thoughts filled your mind for much of the time, imagine how much of your time may be devoted to your obsessive thoughts without your even realizing it. After you've practiced the techniques for a while, you might want to retake this little test to see if your perception of time has become more accurate.

Exercise: Inhale, Exhale, Repeat

Mindful breathing is perhaps the practice most commonly associated with mindfulness—and with good reason: to train yourself to be fully aware of the present moment, you need to have something to place your entire focus on. You could choose anything, really, but there are several advantages to choosing the breath. For one thing, it's free. And it's always conveniently available whenever you choose to pay attention to it. The breath also physically connects you to the world around you. And, when you really watch it closely, you'll discover things about your breathing that you might never have even imagined: its depth and cadence, and how it feels as it moves through your nose and into your lungs as well as inside your chest. In all, it's a terrific object of mindfulness study.

Your initial attempts at mindful breathing should be short. Three minutes is a good place to start, but even this is a long time to remain intently focused on your breath. If you find this too challenging, you can start with just a single minute. Progressively increase your practice periods until you can sit with your breath for fifteen, thirty, or even forty-five minutes. But how long you can sit is less important than sitting regularly. Many people find it helpful to set aside more than one shorter practice period a day, such as once in the morning and again in the evening. Remember that this is your practice; whatever is comfortable for you and gets you closer to your goal of paying attention to the present moment is the right approach for you.

A technique that many people use when beginning a mindful breathing practice is breath counting. We will describe how to do this simple technique, and we recommend your using it when you first begin your practice. Breath counting will help you stay focused when your mind starts to wander. But you can look forward to a time when you can stop counting your breath and simply focus on each inhalation and exhalation as it happens.

As you watch your breathing, you'll pay attention to all of the physical sensations that are part of the process: the rise and fall of your stomach and chest, that cool sensation on your upper lip and inside your nostrils, the feel of pressure in your lungs. As you practice, you will become aware of ever-subtler details in your breathing, making this an even richer exercise.

Your thoughts play a very important role in mindful breathing. As mentioned in chapter 4, you don't have a lot of control over your thoughts, and this fact becomes *very* evident when you start this practice. Thoughts of every stripe will start popping up when you least expect them. They might be OCD-related thoughts or everyday, garden-variety thoughts about the details of your life. You might even have thoughts about the nature of your practice. And this is perfectly fine. However, your job is just to watch those thoughts come and then let them go. This experience can be likened to sitting near a highway after dark, watching the headlights of cars appear in the distance, come toward you, and then fade away in the opposite direction. Your attention will wander from your breath perhaps a thousand or ten-thousand times. When it does, your only job is to gently bring it back to your breath. Do this calmly and with kindness. This gentle persistence is the part of this exercise that fosters compassion for both yourself and others.

- To keep track of your practice, find some kind of timer. A kitchen timer, watch, or cellular phone with an alarm will work—but all of these tend to go off like smoke alarms when the time is up. For a gentler conclusion to your practice, you might search the Internet for simple software applications that are specifically for meditation timing. When they go off, they normally use soft tones or even electronic versions of gongs or temple bells. These will be much less jarring than the scream of your alarm clock.

- Pick a quiet place for your practice in your home or some natural setting. Choose a location that will be more or less free from distracting noises, sights, and smells. You can sit on a cushion on the floor or in a chair, but try to find an arrangement that allows you to sit comfortably with your back straight. Lower your eyelids slightly and direct your gaze at a spot on the floor or ground a few feet in front of you. Don't close your eyes completely because this has a tendency to lead your mind to drift off.

- Start your timer and then take three very deep, very slow breaths. After you exhale the third deep breath, breathe normally, without making any special attempt to control or regulate the rate or depth of your breaths.

- Let your breath fall down into your belly. When your belly is full, let the breath continue to rise into your chest. When you exhale, reverse the process.

- When comfortable with the rhythm of your breath, you can begin the breath-counting exercise. On an inhalation, count "one." Then let your breath exhale naturally. On your next inhalation, count "two." Repeat this process until you come to "ten," counting only when you inhale. Don't worry if you lose count or repeat a number. Just pick a place to begin again.

- After completing a cycle of ten breaths, spend a little while paying attention to any physical sensations you may feel. Notice the mechanics of your breathing, the sensation of the cushion or chair beneath you, the feel of the air against your skin. Listen for any subtle sounds that would otherwise escape you. Pay attention to even the slightest details, such as the feel of your clothing against your skin or the weight of your hair against your collar or shoulders.

- After a period of body awareness, repeat the breath-counting exercise for another cycle of ten breaths.

- All the while, you will notice thoughts popping into your head. When this happens, acknowledge them and let them go. Gently turn your attention back to your breathing. You may find that you can focus more effectively when counting breaths or focusing on physical sensations. Slip into whichever practice works best for you when thoughts arise.

- When your timer goes off, take three more deep, slow breaths. Then allow your eyes to open fully, and return your awareness to the room. You may want to take a few moments to gently stretch or take a short walk if your legs or back became a little tight and fatigued from sitting.

As your practice deepens, you can start following these steps when doing activities other than sitting. You can practice mindful breathing when you're out walking, doing the dishes, or working in the garden. But if you find that mindful breathing tends to relax you to the point of drowsiness, don't try this exercise while driving a car.

Mindful breathing is one of the most effective tools you can use to deal with in-the-moment flare-ups of OCD. By stopping for just a minute, focusing on your breath, and allowing your obsessive thoughts to just fall away naturally, you may be able to stop episodes of OCD before they even get started.

Exercise: Feeding Your OCD

This exercise is somewhat involved, so you should probably have practiced mindfulness work for a little while before you try it. It's not that it's all that hard; as with all the other exercises in this chapter, it just invites things that are already present to come clearly into focus. But it does involve a fair amount of visualization, and has a number of steps that you'll want to have committed to memory before starting—which can be a bit much to handle if you're not used to how this kind of work feels. If you have trouble keeping all of the steps in your mind when trying the exercise, you might want to record the steps on an audio recording device, creating your own guided audio meditation. This can be fun and can make this particular exercise doubly powerful.

Basically, this exercise is about taking a disturbing thought and getting to know it better. Like sitting with a disturbing situation in your ERP work, this might be a little unnerving at first. If you feel that this exercise is too much for you to do alone, just leave it be. You can either come back to it another day or simply do other mindfulness exercises that you are more comfortable with. But part of the goal of this work is for you to learn to recognize a thought as just a thought, something that you can acknowledge and let pass. By physicalizing a distressing thought, you'll learn to look at it in a new way and maybe even learn to appreciate it as a part of you that needs to be treated with kindness and compassion.

- Begin this exercise the same as mindful breathing, in a comfortable spot sitting on a chair or a cushion. Take three deep, slow breaths. Then spend a few minutes concentrating on your breath. If you want, you can go through a few cycles of breath counting.

- After settling into your breathing, allow your mind to focus on some thought that has been troubling you. This could be an OCD-related thought such as "I need to check the knobs on the stove very carefully or I might burn down the house" or "I might lose control of myself when I'm changing my son's diaper and touch him inappropriately." Or it could be some other thought you're wrestling with. Either way, allow it to come clearly into your mind and just let your awareness settle around it.

- As you watch this thought, allow it to take on a shape in your mind. It could be round, square, or jumbled up like a ball of string. Whatever shape it takes is fine. When your thought has a definite shape, allow it to take on a color. Maybe it will be snow white, jet black, fern green, or coffee brown. Let your awareness settle on the color and shape of your distressing thought. Finally, let your thought take on the form of some kind of being. Allow it to have recognizable features: a face with eyes, a nose, ears, and a mouth. Your thought may have arms and legs, wings, or a tail. It may seem friendly or threatening, but just watch it. Know that it is just a thought and it cannot harm you.

- Now that your thought has a form, imagine where it is in your body. Is it floating inside your head or moving around in your chest? Maybe it's at your fingertips or underneath your backside as you sit there. It may be motionless, or it could move around inside you. Whatever it's doing, become aware of it.

- Now invite your thought outside of your body. Don't do this in the spirit of casting it away. Just bring it outside of yourself so that you can take it in with perspective, so that you can see it from a different angle and in a different light. Your thought might sit across the room from you or float over your head. Notice your thought and just let it do what it needs to do.

- Once you've become fully aware of your thought outside your body, ask it the question, "What do you need?" Then just listen to the answer it gives you. When it answers you, think for a moment about what it says. Try to sense whether it has told you what it *really* needs or merely what it wants. You may need to ask it again what it needs. Your thought might tell you that it needs to be certain and safe, or loved and protected. Whatever your thought has to say, just watch and listen.

- Once you know what your thought needs, imagine that you have a boundless supply of whatever that might be. If your thought needs certainty, you can imagine how completely certain you are of the present moment—that you are breathing in and out, and sitting solidly in your room. If your thought needs safety, love, or protection, visualize these things pouring out of you. Invite your thought to you, allowing it to take what it needs from you and imagining that you can provide it easily with whatever will make it whole and well. As you do this, notice whether or not your attitude changes toward your thought. Even if it was very disturbing to you, you may now feel a certain tenderness for it. As you treat your disturbing thought with kindness and compassion, you may find it less frightening, less distressing.

- When you have fed your thought, invite it back inside yourself. Remember that your thought is not something that you *are*. It is something that you *have*. Your goal is not to push it away or get rid of it. Instead, you want to learn how to live with it gently and without judgment, allowing it to come and go effortlessly.

- Once your thought is back inside yourself, return your focus to your breath. Count through a cycle of ten normal breaths, followed by three deep, slow breaths. Then gently open your eyes and allow your attention to come back into the room.

This exercise often takes people by surprise. If you've spent a lot of time struggling with disturbing thoughts, it can seem very strange to not only intentionally spend time with them but also to feed and take care of them. But there is a certain paradoxical wisdom to this kind of visualization. By befriending your disturbing thoughts, you're far less likely to be vexed by them in the future. Instead of threatening, scary manifestations, they may start to seem like scared kids that need a helping hand. As you treat them with kindness and compassion, you may soon start extending the same care and concern to yourself. You may find that you develop a less critical and more accepting view of yourself during times of high anxiety.

One Final Word

As long as you keep it up, your mindfulness practice will benefit you in both your progress with OCD and other areas of your life. But we caution you not to embark on a mindfulness practice just to help you deal with the symptoms of OCD. As mentioned many times in this chapter, the purpose of mindfulness is to pay close attention to the present moment. You'll get the most out of your practice if you do it for no other reason than simply to do it. Any expectations you bring to your practice will become barriers to really experiencing things as they unfold. It's an old joke among meditation students that nothing can ruin the serenity and peace of a period of sitting practice than the sudden intrusion of the thought, "Hey, I'm really doing a great job meditating!" The same is true for the thought, "Boy, I'm really going to get over my OCD by doing all of this good mindfulness work." Instead, just relax and let whatever happens happen. By applying yourself to developing this practice for its own sake, you'll surprise yourself by how much you'll learn about yourself and the world around you.

It Just Kills Me to See You Like This

So far in this book, we've addressed people who actually have OCD. But let's face it: most people with the disorder have their hands full just wrestling with obsessions and performing their compulsive rituals. OCD can be a full-time job—with overtime expected! Choosing to read up on the disorder demonstrates considerable initiative and a willingness to change on the part of someone with OCD. But for every one of these individuals who decides to take back his or her life from the disorder, hundreds more endure helplessly the painful cycle of obsessions and compulsions.

But this doesn't mean they suffer in isolation—far from it. The friends and family members of those with OCD also bear the burden of the disorder, willingly or not. Many loving spouses endure the overwhelming stench of cleaning products in their homes for years, watching helplessly as their mates clean and reclean every surface. And even old and dear friends start "forgetting" to call the one guy in the foursome who always makes them miss their tee time by going back to check the front door a dozen times. If someone in your life is struggling with OCD, this chapter is especially for you.

First, the good news: you're not helpless. There are things you can do to be a better ally and advocate for your loved one, and there are other things you can do to make living with an OCD sufferer more manageable for you and assist in the recovery process. The bad news is, as much as we wish we could, we can't offer a pill or magic wand to "fix" your loved one. Ultimately the decision to do something about OCD is his or hers alone. But when that time comes, this chapter will prepare you to offer the support and encouragement your loved one will need to make real and lasting change.

A Little Knowledge Goes a Long Way

To be as supportive as possible for your loved one with OCD, you'll want to learn as much as you can about the disorder. Remember that OCD is an anxiety disorder, and one of the surest remedies for anxiety is solid fact. The more you know about what OCD is, the less you'll need to worry about what it might be. If you flipped right to this chapter, we suggest you go back and read chapter 1 to get started. The resources you'll find in chapter 8 will help you learn even more. Take the time to do the necessary fact-finding to get a basic level of understanding about this disorder. When you're ready, consulting a mental health professional with specialized knowledge and experi-ence treating OCD can be very helpful. He or she can help you understand your unique situation.

Another useful step is to attend an OCD support group. This is an excellent way to meet firsthand other partners and family members struggling with the same issues as you. This experience can provide a powerful sense that you are not alone in your concerns and struggles, and offer the opportunity to see your loved one's OCD in a more realistic light. See chapter 8 for help finding a support group in your area.

Educating yourself about the disorder will help you respond much more effectively to your loved one with OCD. It will also help you address the concerns, fears, and anxieties of other friends and family members, including children, relatives, and even close friends.

Dealing with Blame and Shame

People who catch colds are so lazy! Haven't they heard of chicken soup and warm jackets? And what about those diabet-ics? The rest of us have normal blood-sugar levels. What's their problem?

Sounds ridiculous, doesn't it? Yet many people with OCD face these kinds of jabs and jeers every day. We've said it before, but it bears repeating: OCD is a neurobehavioral disorder—the result of a complex interaction of genetic, neurobiological, environmental, and psychological factors. Blaming someone with OCD for his or her condition is like blaming somebody for getting struck by lightning. Yes, he or she could have avoided that run to the market for milk on a rainy day, or decided ten years ago to forgo moving to a region known for rain and lightning storms. But that's life. Sometimes bad stuff just happens! It's no one's fault. To assign blame to a person or situation as the "cause" of OCD is similarly naive and shortsighted. As someone who has treated a great many OCD patients, Dr. Hyman has searched for the one true cause of OCD and has been led to this conclusion: OCD is the result of complex genetic, biological, psychological, and environmental "accidents" that are simply too complicated to accurately describe. To assign a single source of blame for this complex of factors resulting in OCD is just unfair and plain wrong. It is neither the fault of the sufferers nor their families. OCD is just something that happens.

So get off the OCD sufferer's back and start learning the facts about the disorder. This will move you past shaming and blaming by helping you confront the mystery, fear, and confusion surrounding this disorder, and it will help you make empowering and constructive choices with respect to your loved one.

Taking Charge

You can begin to make progress by communicating honestly with your loved one about his or her OCD. With his or her permission, you may begin to talk openly about the disorder with family members and others whom you feel are capable of understanding and offering support. However, be prepared: Some of the people close to you may have very strong preconceptions about the cause of your loved one's OCD or the best way for him or her to "get over" it. Don't let yourself be swayed by the myriad of misinformed opinions you will probably encounter, but also try not to force others to see things your way—even if you believe that your viewpoint is factual, well researched, and well reasoned. Even if some fight hard to keep their illusions, this doesn't make them "bad" people. Be persistent in advocating for your loved one, and let others come to terms with him or her in their own time. Remember, as frustrated as you and those around you are with the person with OCD, it is he or she who suffers most from the disorder.

Remember how we mentioned that your loved one's decision to do something about OCD was his or hers alone? This is so true; until this person is ready to change, there's not much you can do to change his or her mind. Yet there are things you can do to support your loved one's recovery from OCD while starting to limit the crippling effects of OCD on family life.

Getting Out of the Enabling Trap

OCD doesn't just disable individuals. It also affects the family as a whole. The endless cycle of obsessions and compulsions often leads to profound changes in the normal patterns of family life to an extent that "normal" family interaction becomes impossible. You may feel the need to sometimes "keep the peace," giving in to OCD's "rules" to even function in the same home as your loved one who has it. What you need to do varies with his or her symptoms. Here are some examples:

- Doing many extra loads of laundry because clothes become "contaminated" from even the thought of their having contacted dirt, germs, or bodily fluids

- Requiring the children to change clothes and shower each and every time they enter the house

- Making special trips home to lock doors, check windows, and so forth

- Constantly reassuring your loved one that he or she has not unknowingly run someone over with the car

- Repeatedly reassuring your loved one that his or her thoughts about others will not cause these people to die, get sick, or be harmed

- Repeatedly reassuring your loved one about the limits of disease transmission

Indeed, family members can become so enmeshed in the disorder that sometimes it appears that the entire family has OCD! The feelings of helplessness, tension, and even anger can be so intense!

If you read this book and others like it, you'll eventually realize that your loved one's OCD is not a choice, but rather a response to internally generated "false alarms" of fear and distress that can scarcely be controlled. However, it's wise to also consider that automatically accommodating OCD's demands may actually fuel rather than help the sufferer's problem. The reason is that, for OCD sufferers, efforts intended to reduce anxiety actually tend to increase it. Remember that reducing anxiety is what compulsions are supposed to do in the first place. Always being reassured by you and others that he or she is safe, healthy, and so on won't give your loved one the incentive he or she needs to learn the exposure and mindfulness skills that can really lead to mastery over discomfort and uncertainty.

Now, if you've engaged in enabling behavior all along, the previous paragraph may sound like a huge relief. "Aha!" you cry. "I knew it all along! I will quit enabling OCD right this very moment!" Not so fast! Keep reading. We're not—and we repeat, *not*—recommending that you and any other family members immediately stop or change anything you're now doing for your loved one with OCD. To stop enabling OCD requires a thoughtful, systematic approach with opportunities and pitfalls along each step of the way. Your goals are to improve how your family functions in the presence of OCD, encourage your loved one to accept treatment for the disorder, and gradually withdraw any OCD-enabling behaviors. Here are the steps to make it happen:

1. Start with a frank discussion with your loved one, preferably with the help of an experienced professional who understands OCD and how to treat it (see chapter 8 for more information). Discuss how your family has participated in your loved one's OCD. Then work together to arrive at a strategy for gradual disengagement.

2. Remain mindful of the fact that the problem is the OCD, not the person who has it. Stay away from blame and anger.

3. Work to bring your loved one to the understanding that the OCD is fed by compulsions and that any "relief" they offer comes at the severe price of

maintaining the destructive, vicious cycle of OCD. Help him or her see the necessity of facing this fact squarely and finding the resolve and courage to set the family free from OCD's demands. This is best accomplished in the context of an agreement among you, your family, and your loved one to work on overcoming OCD together.

4. Work out a clear and consistent plan for family members to gradually break free of OCD's tyrannical "rules" that have so contorted the family's day-to-day life and inadvertently fed the OCD problem. Start with small, manageable changes in routines that may not arouse too much anxiety, such as offering verbal reassurance, and gradually increase the family's "OCD noncompliance" to daily routines that may result in somewhat greater, but manageable, discomfort to the patient. Stick with it with firm resolve, but allow for minor modifications as necessary.

5. If your loved one begins OCD treatment, offer support by being prepared to step back and allow the process to unfold. Treatment for OCD is a highly challenging process that progresses in fits and starts. Be patient and avoid interfering in the process.

The Fallout from No Longer Enabling OCD

While it's important to stop enabling your loved one's OCD, it is very likely that doing so will cause, at least temporarily, an increase in his or her anxiety. You can minimize the impact of your decision to stop enabling OCD by doing it in a way that is gradual, compassionate, and clearly articulated. If your loved one has already decided to work on the OCD, the two of you can collaborate on how you will go about disengaging from his or her compulsions. If professional help is involved, the therapist or counselor will greatly assist in facilitating this process.

However, if your loved one is not ready to seek help, you should still consider untangling yourself from the enabling trap. Here are a few tips to help you make the transition as painlessly as possible:

- Be prepared for the increase in your loved one's anxiety and for a possible increase in OCD symptoms. It may be hard to watch and even harder to live with, but these escalations are sure signs of change. Your loved one's reaction to your new response may range from irritation and uneasiness to rage and incapacitating fear. Stay calm, understanding, and resolved.

- Be honest with your loved one about your intentions. Tell him or her clearly what you plan to do and why. Don't let yourself be lured into arguing about whether or not it's a good decision, though. Be calm and caring, but stick to your guns.

• Consider implementing your disengagement in a gradual, but not overly so, progression. Decrease your participation by perhaps 25 percent each week for a month. Set a date with your loved one to completely stop all enabling; don't negotiate this date after it has been set.

• Politely decline any requests your loved one makes for your help in relieving his or her anxiety. Remember that the only way he or she will ever deal with doubt and uncertainty is by learning to live with it. If you *absolutely* can't refrain from giving reassurance, try only giving it once per day—and work toward eliminating it entirely. Sometimes humor helps relieve the tension of reassurance requests. Responding to requests concerning possible dangers of contamination such as "Are you sure it's okay? Am I really safe?" with "Of course not—you've just contaminated the entire East Coast of the continental USA!" gets the message across.

• Channel your energies previously reserved for OCD toward activities and pursuits that can relieve your stress and enrich your own life. Taking care of yourself enables you to recharge, thus making you a better source of support for your loved one.

• Remember, you are not just the spouse, parent, child, other relative, or friend of someone with OCD. You have other roles and responsibilities in life, and are entitled to attend to these as necessary.

Maintaining Progress

At this point, you've learned a lot about how to make positive changes in your life when you have OCD. You know how and why to do ERP. You've learned the basics of keeping contact with the present moment by using mindfulness skills. And you've found out how to view your thoughts in a new way that can help you live your life for you rather than for your OCD. If you've practiced these skills for a while, you've probably seen some improvements. Your symptoms may have decreased, bringing your confidence to an all-time high. So, what next?

First, the good news: As you work steadily to manage your OCD, you'll start to have more "good" days, days when the Doomsayer seems to have taken a vacation; days when you can work, play, and socialize; days that make life rich, purposeful, and fun. When you first started working on your OCD, you might only have had good days every once in a while, but the longer you practice the techniques in this book, the more frequent your good days may become. A great deal of psychological research points to these techniques as offering you the best possible chance to get better.

And now the bad news: Well, it's not really bad news. It's more like "the way it is" news. Some days, you will experience OCD symptoms. It's going to happen. There's something about the unique combination of biological, social, and psychological factors that make you who you are that leads to these symptoms. They don't define who you are or what you can do with your life, but it's unlikely that they'll ever totally go away. You'll have bad days from time to time. In fact, you *need* bad days to test your progress with the disorder; they are important and necessary checkpoints on your path. Make it your goal to acknowledge your slip and then let it go, continuing to work toward a life unburdened by OCD.

Distinguishing Lapse from Relapse

You'll have an easier time dealing with bad days if you know what they might look like. We describe them as either involving lapses or relapses. There is a big difference between the two.

Lapses are relatively small, transitory flare-ups of your OCD symptoms. They probably won't last very long, and you'll generally have a good idea of what might have caused them. Just about any stressful period in your life can be a likely suspect: getting married or divorced, changing jobs, having a child, moving, or becoming injured or ill—any major event with strong negative or positive feelings associated with it. Lapses are a normal part of the almost tidal flow of your symptoms, which will seem to come and go regularly. As long as you don't get too caught up in them, lapses won't mean much in the course of your recovery. Once the stressful event they're related to resolves, the lapse, too, should taper off, and you won't have lost any of the treatment gains that you've built up over time.

Relapses are much less common than lapses. These are periods when your OCD symptoms return to pretreatment levels. You can usually relate relapses to a very significant stress or disruption in your life—a loss of a major source of support, a traumatic event, a serious economic or professional setback. Relapses are usually complicated by additional factors such as alcohol or drug abuse. In the majority of cases, relapses occur when people with OCD go off of prescribed anti-OCD medication. If you ever think you are experiencing a period of relapse, we strongly suggest that you seek the help of a qualified professional with experience treating OCD.

Stepping Up to the Bad Days

There are quite a few things you can do to minimize lapses and help prevent relapses. It will help you tremendously to start paying attention to many of these things now, before you start experiencing bad days. As your grandmother might have told you (if she was one of those grandmothers who is forever spouting pithy folk wisdom), an ounce of prevention is worth a pound of cure.

Some of the lapse- and relapse-prevention steps that follow in this section are good to keep in mind whenever you can. However, this first one is not one of those; this one you need to remember at all times—period. If you are taking anti-OCD prescription medication, you must never go off of your meds without first consulting your physician. This holds true no matter how you feel or what's happening with your symptoms. Consult your doctor about every aspect of your treatment. Also, if you happen to be getting good results with medication, talk to your doctor about incorporating behavioral care (such as the ERP and mindfulness techniques in this book) into your overall program. Medication can be a great help to you, but you probably won't be able to make OCD go away forever with medication alone. The behavioral work you've learned in this book will help retrain your brain to deal with OCD so you can make progress on the things that really matter to you in your life.

In your progress with OCD, as in all things, try to be kind to yourself. Remember that lapses and relapses are a part of living with OCD. Try not to think of them as failures. You should instead regard them as opportunities to challenge yourself and the progress you've made with the disorder. When you do have a bad day, accept it gently and with compassion for yourself. Get in touch with, or just be with, your obsessions and compulsions—think of this as a kind of mini-ERP in which you expose yourself to OCD itself. Get familiar with your experiences. Next time OCD symptoms happen, you'll be better prepared to just let go of unwanted thoughts and feelings.

Even though occasional slips in progress are normal, they are still significant. Don't ignore them or pretend that they don't matter. Being mindful of little slips by watching them is the best way to stop them from turning into big slips and relapses.

You should also be on the lookout for the tendency to replace big, obvious compulsive rituals with smaller, more discreet ones. If you formerly checked the door ten times before leaving the house, for example, you may start just touching the doorknob three times on your way out. Although these little compulsions may seem like a step in the right direction and attract less attention from your friends and family, they still reinforce your dependence on compulsions and their supposed benefits. Be as diligent with little compulsions as you are with big ones. Include them in your ERP work; be mindful of them, doing whatever it takes, over time, to shift your behavior away from *any* dependence on compulsive rituals.

What about OCD-related problems that are not part of the cycle of obsessions and compulsions? Depression is probably the most common co-occurring problem. Especially if you've made strides in your work with OCD, you may start wondering what your life might have been like if you had started this work sooner, if you had been able to live more years without carrying around the disorder. Again, the first thing you'll want to remember is to be kind to yourself. Everyone suffers, and no life is free from adversity. We are historical creatures, for better or worse. Our past cannot be changed, only elaborated upon. That's what you're doing now, and you can feel very proud of this. So how do you cope with feelings of depression? The best way is to get moving. Do what you enjoy or what will help you accomplish your short- and long-term goals. You'll be amazed at how fleeting feelings of depression become once you're active, engaged, and working toward the things that matter to you. If you feel that your feelings of depression are a more serious problem in your life, talk to your therapist or doctor about them.

Finally, remember that your goal is to live a rich, purposeful, and fulfilling life, whether or not you have OCD symptoms. This may mean that you need to work some to reduce your symptoms, but it definitely doesn't mean that you need a cure. Keep this in mind as you set your expectations for your OCD

work. You're living your life right here, right now. If you keep
this in mind, ultimately you won't have good days and bad days;
you'll have only vital days, in which you take in and experience
everything life has to offer, and make choices that move you in
directions that matter to you.

Common Challenges in OCD Recovery

If you find that ERP, mindfulness work, and your new take on
your thoughts are not getting you where you want to go, you
might've run aground on some of the more common obstacles
that come up for people working on OCD. Paying attention to
the following traps might speed up your progress and keep you
from getting stuck along the way.

Keeping Well and Away from the Edge

As mentioned back in chapter 1, people with OCD tend to
be of above-average intelligence, so we won't waste your valuable time telling you that you need to eat healthfully, exercise,
or do something about that white-knuckle problem if your
stress level is off the charts. If you don't already know this stuff,
you've probably got a spaceship parked in your driveway. If this
is the case, know that we Earthlings mean you no harm—and
know that there are about a million good books that can help
you figure out a way of eating, moving, and calming down that
works for you. Go read a couple! If they sound ridiculous, go
read some other ones. If you've worked on your OCD using
the techniques in this book but have gotten nowhere, consider

your diet, exercise habits, and stress level. Would it help you reach your goals if you actually ate three meals a day instead of starving yourself until two o'clock in the afternoon? What if you skipped that third cup of coffee and the accompanying jitters? Would you relax and sleep better if you took a walk in the evenings? What if you turned off your phone, ignored your e-mail, and listed to Chopin for an hour each day? Nothing we could mention here will work for everybody all of the time. Only you can figure out what combination of things works for your body. But we can tell you this: making progress with OCD will be much easier if you take care of yourself, but it may be impeded if you don't.

And do we need to remind you that excessive drinking or drug use can complicate your recovery efforts? If you're engaging in either of these behaviors at the moment, chances are that you're, at least in part, self-medicating for your OCD symptoms. Before you set out to make significant changes to your OCD behaviors, you'll need to get your substance issues under control. This is especially true if you're receiving or considering medical treatment for OCD. Drugs and alcohol may neutralize or interfere with your prescribed medication's therapeutic effects. You also run the risk of experiencing dangerous drug interactions and complications. If you think you have a problem with substance abuse, seek out a qualified professional to help you make a recovery plan.

The Problem of Avoidance

Some psychologists believe that *all* emotional disorders have the common root of experiential avoidance, a basic unwillingness to endure emotionally painful experience. According to this point of view, all disordered behavior—such as OCD, general anxiety disorder, depression, and post-traumatic stress disorder (PTSD)—serves to protect the sufferer from some other, more fearful and painful experience. (This viewpoint is characteristic of the new treatment approach mentioned earlier called acceptance and commitment therapy [ACT]. To learn more about ACT, see the further references in chapter 8.)

Whether you buy this or not, it's certain that persistent avoidance can greatly hinder your progress with OCD. Pay close attention to anything you do that might be avoidant. If you have contamination OCD, this might include a reluctance to handle certain things or engage in activities that might bring you in contact with "dirty" objects such as doorknobs, water fountains, and public washrooms. If you have problems with checking, perhaps you have set it up so that your spouse always leaves the house last and is thus the one to lock the door instead of you. Maybe you go a block out of your way to avoid driving by a school because you obsess over the possibility of running over a child who dashes into the street. Of course, these are just a few of the literally countless varieties of avoidance that you might engage in. Most of these appear to be harmless ways to avoid triggering situations that could tie you up in a compulsion that could literally ruin your day. However benign, the more of these anxiety-provoking situations you avoid, the more vulnerable you are to future lapses in your recovery should you find yourself in a stressful situation. When you realize you've been avoiding something, put it on your ERP hierarchy list and get to work. Once you find that you can engage with the object or situation that you formerly avoided, look for the next thing.

Persistently rooting out your avoidance tendencies will greatly help you in your progress with OCD.

You don't need to interact with the physical world to engage in experiential avoidance. One particularly insidious form of avoidance is called *protective distraction*, or *blocking*. In this variety of avoidance, you use your mind to pull back from a painful experience even while going through the motions of carrying it out with your body. This stumbling block is particularly problematic when it comes up while you're doing ERP. Say, for example, that you have contamination OCD, and you have a strong fear of touching dirt. You choose to engage in ERP and finally work your way up to sticking your fingers into an actual cup of garden soil. You really get in there and squish your fingers around in God knows what, but all the while, you imagine that you're handling pure, sterile sand. What do you know? This is much easier than you thought!

But guess again. Your blocking thoughts literally prevent the ERP from doing its work. And you just dipped your fingers into that peaty sludge for nothing. If you're going to do ERP, let down your internal defenses and really do it. Allow your thoughts to sit with even the most disturbing consequences of whatever you're doing. Allow your anxiety to rise and fall away naturally. If you find it too hard to be with all of the possible catastrophes that you link to a particular exposure behavior, go back to the previous step on your distress hierarchy and work there until you can move forward. But do move forward. It's critical to your progress with OCD that you learn to recognize and let go of those situations you usually avoid.

If It Waddles and Quacks, It's a Duck

After you've worked on OCD for a while and made some progress, you'll very likely encounter situations in which you engage in a compulsion and muse, "Maybe this time it's not my OCD." Let's say, for example, that you struggle with the obsessive thought that if you chop carrots in the kitchen, you will somehow lose control and harm your spouse or child with your knife. You've used the techniques in this book for a while. You've become mindful of this thought when it pops up, and you've recognized that just because you think it, that doesn't necessarily mean it will happen. And you've done a number of ERP sessions, working your way up to cutting carrots for five minutes while your loved one sits in a chair across the room. At first, any action like this made your anxiety spiral. But gradually it has gone down, and now you can more or less cut the carrots without distress. All of a sudden, though, the thought hits you that maybe all of the other times you practiced ERP were about OCD, but this time it's different—today it's not OCD, and you truly are a psychopathic killer. As you cut, you can almost feel the knife edging out of your hand, pointing itself at your loved one. This time the danger hasn't been manufactured by your OCD. This time it's real.

Sorry, but it's not real this time, and it won't be real the next time either. Sometimes, especially if external life stressors are high, it's all too easy for the mind to slip into the familiar "What if...?!" mode and make well-worn OCD thoughts into new signals for possible disasters. If you want a very simple rule of thumb, always assume that any thought that resembles any of your previous OCD thoughts is still OCD.

Another kind of denial occurs when you tell yourself that you're engaging in a compulsion for the greater good, to keep the people around you safe from harm. This is a very sad kind of denial. It numbs you to the very real pain that the people who care about you feel as a result of your OCD. At the same time, it gives you a false sense of pride and accomplishment, making you into something of a martyr. You go on washing, counting, or checking, thinking with pride that you're protecting the people you care about. And since none of them seems to be dying, you must be doing something right. But the truth is that they're suffering. And you're suffering—all needlessly. And the longer you deny that fact, the more pain you and your loved ones will have to endure. At all costs, martyr denial needs to be recognized and dealt with. The best way to come to terms with this and other kinds of denial is to take time to sit with your doubts. Watch them for as long as it takes. Ask yourself serious questions about what you might be trying to avoid. Chances are, you may discover the truth of it all: that you're not really protecting your loved ones by going to such exhausting lengths. You're protecting yourself. Remember that challenging your thoughts to reduce OCD's impact upon you and your family's daily lives is the best "protection" you can offer your family. Letting go of denial is the first step toward that end.

Social Isolation and Family Conflicts

Here's the bottom line: You'll probably have a hard time pouring a bowl of cereal while feeling isolated, lonely, and disconnected. You sure as hell won't be able to do anything as complex and demanding as making progress with OCD. You need people in your life who understand what you're going through and can be there for you when you need a shoulder to lean on. It's great if your intimate friends and family can lend you this kind of support, but sometimes they just can't—and that might just be the way it is. If this is the case, you should know that there are literally hundreds of OCD support groups across the country and around the world that can help. When you connect with one of these groups, you'll find caring people just like you who know what you're going through. Having this kind of support can be an invaluable aid as you work toward your goals. The group you find may also be open to your immediate family, providing them with welcome support too. Take a look at the resources in chapter 8 for help in locating an OCD support group near you.

It won't come as a surprise to you that a chaotic, stressful family life will hinder your OCD work. What may surprise you, though, is that any progress you make on the disorder may actually destabilize your family life rather than make it smoother. When your symptoms were in full swing, your loved ones had to adjust to your behavior. Now that you've made some improvements, they'll need to adjust again. It's very likely that your loved ones will delight in the new you, but it's not unheard of, either, for them to feel that you don't need them when they're no longer enlisted to enable your OCD behavior. It's possible that a family member might actually resent that you've let go of some parts of your OCD. Depending on your situation, the process of reinventing your life after OCD can be joyful or challenging. We hope it's the former, but if it's the latter, we urge you to seek a qualified family therapist to help with the transition. Please see chapter 8 for information on finding a qualified professional.

Further Help for Stubborn Cases

So far in this section, we've covered a number of issues that might prevent you from getting the results you want for your OCD work. But what do you do if nothing seems to do the trick or if none of these issues seems to apply to your situation? Think about this: What would you do if you needed a new transmission in your car and a new roof on your house? And what if, at the same time, you needed to get your dog spayed and have a cavity filled? Well, you might do one of these tasks yourself, maybe even two, if you were very broadly skilled. But eventually you'd need to call a professional. There are thousands of people out there who make it their life's work to help people like you make better lives for themselves. If your best efforts to help yourself haven't paid off, it's time to get in touch with a doctor or therapist who can work with you to help you implement the approaches discussed in this book, approaches that are known to help reduce suffering from OCD.

One option to explore with your doctor is medication. There are a number of new medicines and medication strategies that have shown great promise for reducing OCD symptoms. We mentioned a little about the basic approaches to OCD medication in chapter 1, and a more detailed discussion of these options is beyond the scope of this book. But we can point you in the direction of a qualified professional (see chapter 8).

You might be apprehensive about considering medication for your OCD problem. This is normal. It might help to know that most medications, appropriately administered and taken as directed, will at least offer some relief for most people with OCD, and there are many choices available to your doctor should you not respond to any single medication trial. OCD medications are not addictive, so you can stop taking them anytime you and your doctor decide it's best to do so (in some cases, tapering dosages is required). It may be the case that you'll only get relief from OCD when taking medication, so you might need to take meds indefinitely; but this is a small price to pay for the chance to live a fuller and richer life.

Finding Out More

If your path to breaking free from OCD is a journey, this chapter will help you pack. What follows is a discussion, by no means exhaustive, of resources that may help you locate competent professional help, learn more about OCD, and connect with sources of support in your community.

Finding and Working with Doctors and Therapists

There are many kinds of mental health clinicians out there, such as psychiatrists, psychologists, and clinical social workers. So choosing a clinician to help you with OCD can be very confusing indeed. As you search for the right professional to help you, it's important to familiarize yourself with the different kinds of

practitioners and the services they offer. However, as you read
on, keep in mind that the most important qualification to look
for in a physician or therapist is solid experience treating OCD.
No degree or license substitutes for the kinds of insights that
come from actually helping people just like you make progress
against the disorder.

Overall, in choosing a clinician, remember an important
point we made in the earliest chapters of this book: all mental
disorders, including OCD, result from a complex interaction of both biological and environmental (learned attitudes,
beliefs, and behaviors based in psychological principles) factors.
What this means is that most people with OCD will need to
work with not one but two professionals: one for the biological causes of mental disorders, usually a medical doctor, and
another expert in the psychological/environmental factors, such
as a psychotherapist. Medical doctors specially trained in diag-
nosing and treating the biological basis of psychiatric and psychological problems are known as *psychiatrists* and are licensed
to prescribe medications to alleviate OCD symptoms. On the
other hand, *psychotherapists* are experts in the cognitive and
behavioral influences impacting mental health problems, and
hold either a doctoral degree (clinical psychologists with Ph.D.,
Psy.D., or Ed.D. degrees) or a master's degree (MSW, MFT,
or MHC), as well as a license from the state they work in to
practice mental health care. (For a thorough explanation of the
roles and qualifications of mental health providers, we recommend taking a look at the book *Getting Help: The Complete and
Authoritative Guide to Self-Assessment and Treatment of Mental
Health Problems*, by Jeffrey Wood (New Harbinger 2007).

Master's-level clinicians include marriage and family therapists (MFTs), mental health counselors (MHCs), and clinical

social workers (LCSWs), all of whom provide psychotherapy services to the public. However, one cannot and should not assume that a member of any of these mental health professions has gone through the basic professional preparation to be qualified to diagnose and treat OCD effectively using the proven methods described in this book. Such competence often requires years of specific focus and specialized training in the methods of CBT to treat OCD, which far too few therapists of any professional group have. "Yikes!" you're probably thinking, "What do I do now?"

First, it's a good idea to visit the website of the Obsessive Compulsive (OC) Foundation, http://www.ocfoundation.org, which maintains a list of psychiatrists and therapists claiming to have additional knowledge and experience in OCD treatment. Because the OC Foundation does not specifically research the credentials and qualifications of every doctor and therapist on its referral list, you'll still want to get such information on anyone you contact. The Obsessive Compulsive Information Center of the Madison Institute of Medicine (http://www.miminc.org/aboutocic.html), the Anxiety Disorders Association of America (ADAA, http://www.adaa.org), and the Association for Behavioral and Cognitive Therapies (ABCT, http://www.abct.org) also maintain lists of therapists who have indicated special interest in treating OCD.

If you live in or around a major metropolitan area, chances are that you're not far from an experienced OCD clinician. However, if there are no specialist practitioners in your area, you may wish to locate the OCD or CBT specialist nearest you and discuss doing CBT remotely, for example, over the telephone or using video-conferencing technology over the Internet. While far from ideal, this can be a viable option for some patients with mild to moderate OCD symptoms living where access to proper care is limited. Sometimes, just talking to a professional who really understands your OCD problem can provide the necessary encouragement to try out the proven strategies on your own. However, since the effectiveness of these remote methods of providing care has not been conclusively established, you will not find these options widely available.

Certainly, those patients with limited access to a qualified specialist in CBT for OCD will benefit from using one of the well-established self-help books featuring a step-by-step approach to doing CBT. One such book is Dr. Hyman's *The OCD Workbook* (New Harbinger 2005). If you have worked with a therapist for a while who does not specialize in OCD and CBT but whom you really like, you may want to request that he or she "coach" you in carrying out the procedures for self-administered CBT described in that book. Some, but obviously not all, therapists may be willing to take on this advisory role in your ongoing care.

For people with severe OCD who have not responded to standard outpatient treatment, an option is to explore one of many excellent centers throughout the United States that offer inpatient or intensive outpatient care. Once again, the OC Foundation is a great resource for locating such programs.

When starting to actually screen clinicians or programs, you'll want to have an idea of what you're getting yourself into before committing to any course of treatment. Though you may be reluctant to do so, don't hesitate to ask any prospective treatment provider about his or her professional credentials, licensing, and professional affiliations. At the bare minimum, that professional must hold a state license verifying completion of the minimum education requirements for licensure and accountability to a professional board for matters of conduct and competency. But don't be awed by credentials. Remember, a master's-level counselor with considerable experience and expertise in treating OCD may be much better able to help you than a general psychologist with limited clinical experience with OCD.

Ask the professional what methods of treatment he or she proposes. You can assume that a psychiatrist will focus on medication, although you can and should ask about concurrent CBT with a therapist experienced in treating OCD. If psychiatrist is not, at least, familiar with CBT for OCD, or dismisses it completely with a broad brush for all OCD patients, that should be a strong signal to move on. Or, psychiatrists who tell you, "I can do that (CBT)!" are probably overestimating their skill level (few psychiatrists have training in CBT) or are too inexperienced with CBT to know that they don't know enough. As for psychologists and other therapists, it is vital that they have significant training and experience in CBT, as well as familiarity with techniques similar to the ones in this book. You should specifically ask about ERP, which is still considered the gold-standard behavioral treatment for OCD. If the professional you're interviewing dismisses or doesn't know about ERP, you probably should consider looking elsewhere.

You certainly should ask all professionals you contact about their direct experience with OCD: How many clients with the disorder have they treated? How many are under their care now? Where and when did they receive training in OCD treatment? A good answer here points to specific clinical training in anxiety-disorder care along with ongoing case supervision during graduate school or subsequent postdoctoral training. It's a big plus if the therapist attended and completed the Behavioral Training

Institute offered by the OC Foundation (http://www.ocfounda-tion.org) to train professionals in using ERP with OCD patients. You might even ask whether OCD has personally touched the professional's life, either rendering him- or herself a sufferer or the friend or family member of one. That's a big plus too. Chances are, a professional's personal experience with OCD will translate into a stronger sense that your daily challenge will be felt and understood.

Finally, you should explore your professional's personal stance on OCD treatment. How does he or she feel about medication? Exercise caution if the professional expresses strong opinions that medication is either inappropriate or dangerous, or the opposite, that medication is the "silver bullet" that will solve all of your problems. Your best bet will be someone who believes in a combined-care approach including both medication and cognitive-behavioral care. Since any treatment you undertake should include ERP, you might ask whether the professional is willing to leave the office to accompany you when conducting in vivo exposure work. You can also inquire about whether he or she can offer telephone consultation and support if you need it between sessions.

Connecting with Others: Support Groups

There are several types of support groups available for people suffering from OCD. Some groups are professionally assisted, highly structured, and therapeutic in nature. Other support groups are informative and provide a supportive, informal, and empathetic environment for people coping with OCD. They are often led and organized by fellow OCD sufferers.

The first type of support group is the mutual support group. This type of group is run by OCD sufferers and is usually held once or twice per month. Typically, the individuals leading the group have recovered from their OCD and are presently managing their symptoms. Some groups have mental health professionals attend in an advisory capacity to answer questions and provide assistance. In these meetings, participants may discuss specific topics such as medication, symptoms, or CBT. The goal of these support groups is informational rather than therapeutic; however, they encourage open sharing by attendees about the challenges facing the OCD sufferer. These groups usually welcome family members and encourage them to attend. They also strongly encourage confidentiality among attendees. Mutual support groups usually are held at a public facility such as a local school or church, and there's usually no fee except sometimes for the use of the room or for refreshments.

The second kind of group is the G.O.A.L. (Giving Obsessive Compulsive Another Lifestyle) group. The original G.O.A.L. group was started by psychologist Dr. Jon Grayson and a recovered person with OCD, in 1981 in Philadelphia. The purpose was to prevent relapse by offering continued support in a group context to people with OCD in their ongoing ERP work. A G.O.A.L. group is professionally assisted. This means that a therapist is present at every meeting, but his or her job is just to provide accurate information about OCD and coach the group leader and attendees in the G.O.A.L. group process. The group is run by its members. A manual and video are available from the OC Foundation (http://www.ocfoundation.org) outlining how to organize and conduct this type of group.

While there are many options for support, in your search for a support group near you, don't be surprised if the nearest group turns out to be hundreds of miles away. Unfortunately, there is a huge unmet need for support groups for patients and family members with OCD in almost every community. It's not clear why this is the case. It appears that, for perhaps several reasons, people with OCD are much less likely to form and attend support groups than people with, say, diabetes or asthma, or bereavement issues or depression. Little research actually exists to understand why this is so, but Dr. Hyman's experience points to the confusion, secrecy, shame, and embarrassment often accompanying OCD, which may result in an extreme reluctance to share or discuss an OCD problem in a public forum, regardless of how "safe" such an environment may be. Also, many OCD patients struggling with their symptoms may fear that hearing about the fears of others will somehow cause them to "contract" others' OCD fears, leaving them in worse shape than before attending. This fear is largely unfounded and should not discourage someone from benefiting from an OCD support group.

If there is no OCD support group in your community, consider starting your own. While it can be challenging, it can also be highly rewarding. The OC Foundation (http://www.ocfoun dation.org) and the Anxiety Disorders Association of America (ADAA, http://www.adaa.org) are good places to begin learning the how-tos of starting and sustaining an OCD support group in your community.

OCD Support on the Internet

The lack of a functioning OCD support group in your community does not mean you're out of luck. With just a few clicks of your mouse, you can find ample, free OCD support on the Internet. In addition to a large general list for discussing OCD's effects and treatment, there are smaller support lists for family members, parents, teens, children, and people with specific symptoms. You can find a list of these groups at the OC Foundation website (http://www.ocfoundation.org) or the ADAA website (http://www.adaa.org). You can join one or several online groups, reading the vast array of postings and contributing to the discussion as you feel the need.

One caveat before venturing into the world of online OCD support groups: Think of online chat as a huge OCD support group with thousands of people in the room, all speaking at the same time. As such, it can be quite overwhelming. Every imaginable situation in dealing with OCD is open to full view by others, so if you ever thought you were alone with your problem and had the worst situation imaginable, that notion will soon be put to rest. Be forewarned that, despite being moderated for content, on most sites almost anything goes. So be prepared to read about every conceivable "flavor" of OCD imaginable. However, if you keep chatting, it's very likely that you will eventually meet your OCD "twin," which can be quite helpful to you. But, should you read about some viewpoint or treatment approach that doesn't jibe with your present view on OCD or is very inconsistent with your present treatment—for example, the notion that having intrusive, aggressive "bad thoughts" is a sign of "repressed aggression" and requires "past-life regression" to eradicate it—discuss it with a trusted mental health professional who, preferably, has significant expertise in OCD treatment so you can put any divergent views in their proper context and perspective. Here are some of the more helpful online chat sites:

OCD Support

This is an e-mail–based online community chat site with membership of more than 2,400. It brings OCD sufferers together through e-mail and is skillfully moderated by Wendy Mueller, a recovered OCD sufferer. Expert advice is provided by Michael Jenike, MD (a Harvard professor who heads the Scientific Advisory Board of the OC Foundation); James Claiborn, Ph.D. (expert in behavior therapy and member of the Scientific Advisory Board of the OC Foundation); and Dr. Jon Grayson (a specialist in CBT for OCD from Philadelphia). For additional information about this chat site, please contact Ms. Mueller at wmueller@roadrunner.com. The subscription address is OCD-Support-subscribe@yahoogroups.com, and the Web address is http://groups.yahoo.com/group/OCD-Support.

Stuck in a Doorway Online Forum

This is an excellent, moderated online chat site for OCD sufferers, based in the United Kingdom. It has a rather large number of sufferers of primarily obsessional OCD, and is ably moderated with compassion and solid information. Visit http://www.stuckinadoorway.co.uk.

Crazyboards

This is another moderated site that promotes very frank discussions of issues related to a variety of psychiatric problems, including OCD. According to the moderators, "This isn't your usual support site. ... You won't find that your every post is responded to with feigned warm fuzziness and cyber-hugs. A lot of other sites place great importance on making sure people are not offended or 'triggered.' We don't. ... Everyone is encouraged to say what they need to say and not worry about what effect it may have on others." Users have reported that this is a helpful site, but be forewarned. You can check it out at http://www.crazyboards.org/forums.

Information Websites

The following websites offer solid, accurate information about what OCD is and how it's treated. These should be your first stop for the most up-to-date and accurate information about OCD, plus links to other authoritative websites:

Obsessive Compulsive Foundation
http://www.ocfoundation.org

Anxiety Disorders Association of America
http://www.adaa.org

U.S. National Library of Medicine
http://www.nlm.nih.gov/medlineplus/
obsessivecompulsivedisorder.html

Awareness Foundation for OCD & Related Disorders
http://www.ocdawareness.com

OCD Resource Center of Florida
http://www.ocdhope.com (Dr. Hyman's website)

Further Reading

There are many books that you might find helpful as you work toward building a better life with OCD. Here are just a few that you might find particularly helpful and inspiring. You can always check in the reference section of any truly helpful book for referrals to additional titles that might interest you.

Books on OCD

Of course, we will first steer you to Dr. Hyman's "big book" with Cherry Pedrick, *The OCD Workbook: Your Guide to Breaking Free from Obsessive-Compulsive Disorder* (New Harbinger 2005). Now in its second edition, this classic volume has sold more than a hundred thousand copies and has helped countless people just like you. The workbook has very detailed exercises for all kinds of OCD and has been recommended widely by therapists working with those struggling with OCD. It also includes expanded information on medications for OCD. If you only read one other OCD book, this should be it.

If you're looking for sound, cognitive behavioral techniques specifically for your variety of OCD, we recommend the following additional New Harbinger titles: *Overcoming Compulsive*

Checking: Free Your Mind from OCD (2004) and *Overcoming Compulsive Washing: Free Your Mind from OCD* (2005), by Paul Munford; and *Overcoming Obsessive Thoughts: How to Gain Control of Your OCD* (2005), by Christine Purdon and David Clark. These titles delve deeply into the particulars of the variety of OCD discussed, offering effective, step-by-step techniques for making and maintaining progress. If you want more information about primarily obsessional OCD, another book we recommend is Lee Baer's *The Imp of the Mind: Exploring the Silent Epidemic of Obsessive Bad Thoughts* (Plume 2002), which is a popular and thorough treatment of the topic of intrusive thoughts.

If you have a family member with OCD, you may want to take a look at *Loving Someone with OCD: Help for You and Your Family* (New Harbinger 2005), by Karen Landsman, Kathleen Rupertus, and Cherry Pedrick. This book offers a very detailed discussion of how best to understand and care for someone in your life who struggles with OCD. A book that can be of great help to you if a child in your life is struggling with OCD is *Helping Your Child with OCD: A Workbook for Parents of Children with Obsessive-Compulsive Disorder* (New Harbinger 2003), by Lee Fitzgibbons and Cherry Pedrick. *Stop Obsessing! How to Overcome Your Obsessions and Compulsions* (Bantam 2001), by Edna Foa and Reid Wilson, offers still another proven, effective approach.

You can find an in-depth, systematic self-help approach to compulsive hoarding in *Overcoming Compulsive Hoarding: Why You Save and How You Can Stop* (New Harbinger 2004), by Fugen Neziroglu, Jerome Bubrick, and Jose Yaryura-Tobias. Likewise, *Buried in Treasures: Help for Compulsive Acquiring, Saving, and Hoarding* (Oxford University Press 2007), by

David F. Tolin, Randy O. Frost, and Gail S. Steketee, outlines a scientifically based program for helping compulsive hoarders dig their way out of the clutter and chaos of their homes.

Books on OCD in Children

Because this book is not specifically geared toward the diagnosis and treatment of OCD in children, many of you may need some guidance on where to turn for help and information. *Helping Your Child with OCD: A Workbook for Parents of Children with Obsessive-Compulsive Disorder* (New Harbinger 2003), by Lee Fitzgibbons and Cherry Pedrick, is very worthwhile, as is *Talking Back to OCD: The Program that Helps Kids and Teens Say "No Way"—and Parents Say "Way to Go"* (Guilford Press 2007), by John S. March. Both books contain useful skills for both children and adolescents with OCD that can help them take control of their OCD. They also give helpful tools and techniques for parents who want to be more effective in helping their children.

Books on Acceptance and Mindfulness Approaches

If you are interested in furthering your understanding of mindfulness and acceptance approaches to mental health disorders, including OCD, the best introduction for general readers is *Get Out of Your Mind and Into Your Life: The New Acceptance and Commitment Therapy* (New Harbinger 2005), by Steven Hayes with Spencer Smith. This book is about acceptance and commitment therapy (ACT), the newest, so-called "third wave" of cognitive behavioral therapy that is gaining ground as an effective treatment approach for anxiety disorders, including OCD. Because ACT views mental health problems differently than most other psychotherapy models, this workbook is not "for" any specific disorder. Instead, it is a general introduction to doing ACT that will help anyone who gives it a serious read. You can also take a look at *The Mindfulness and Acceptance Workbook for Anxiety* (New Harbinger 2007), by John Forsyth and Georg Eifert. This book adapts ACT principles to the whole scope of anxiety disorders, including OCD. Since research is in progress that applies ACT to OCD, stay tuned in the next year or two for a book that specifically applies ACT principles to OCD. You can always keep up on new ACT book releases through New Harbinger's website, http://www.newharbinger. com, or the Association for Contextual Behavioral Science website, http://www.contextualpsychology.org.

If you'd like to delve deeper into the mindfulness area, there are countless terrific books that you can check out. Of course, there are the famous titles by Jon Kabat-Zinn: *Full Catastrophe Living* (Piatkus Books 2001), *Wherever You Go, There You Are: Mindfulness Meditation in Everyday Life* (Hyperion 2005), and *Coming to Our Senses: Healing Ourselves and the World Through Mindfulness* (Hyperion 2006). These are classics, not to be missed by anyone who wants a firm grounding in the secular tradition of mindfulness. Ellen Langer's *Mindfulness* (Addison Wesley 1990) and Thich Nhat Hanh's *The Miracle of Mindfulness* (Beacon Press 1999) are also outstanding volumes in the field.

For an application of mindfulness to the reduction of anxiety, we very strongly recommend *Calming Your Anxious*

Mind: How Mindfulness and Compassion Can Free You from Anxiety, Fear, and Panic (New Harbinger 2007), by Jeffrey Brantley. This book offers a simple and clear approach to building a mindfulness practice that can lead to great progress with anxiety disorders such as OCD. Dr. Brantley's style is warm, friendly, and engaging. If you are looking for some easy, interesting practices to add to your daily mindfulness routine, you might also take a look at his *Five Good Minutes* series of books coauthored by Wendy Millstine (New Harbinger).

References

Abramowitz, J. S. 1997. Effectiveness of psychological and pharmacological treatments for obsessive-compulsive disorder: a quantitative review. *Journal of Consulting and Clinical Psychology* 65:44–52.

Barlow, D. 2004. *Anxiety and Its Disorders.* 2nd ed. New York: Guilford Press.

Baxter, L. R., J. M. Schwartz, K. S. Bergman, M. P. Szuba, B. H. Guze, J. C. Mazziotta, A. Alazraki, C. E. Selin, H. K. Ferng, P. Munford et al. at Department of Psychiatry, UCLA School of Medicine. 1992. Caudate glucose metabolic rate changes with both drug and behavior therapy for obsessive-compulsive disorder. *Archives of General Psychiatry* 49(9).

Freeston, M. H., R. Ladouceur, F. Gagnon, N. Thibodeau, J. Rhéaume, H. Letarte, and A. Bujold. 1997. Cognitive-behavioral treatment of obsessive thoughts: a controlled study. *Journal of Consulting and Clinical Psychology* 65:405–13.

Grayson, J. 2004. *Freedom from Obsessive-Compulsive Disorder: A Personalized Recovery Program for Living with Uncertainty.* New York: The Berkeley Publishing Group.

Hayes, S., and S. Smith. 2005. *Get Out of Your Mind and Into Your Life: The New Acceptance and Commitment Therapy.* Oakland, CA: New Harbinger Publications, Inc.

Kabat-Zinn, J. 2003. Mindfulness-based interventions in context: past, present, and future. *Clinical Psychology: Science and Practice* 10(2):144–56.

Milton, J. 2003. *Paradise Lost.* New York: Penguin Classics.

Rachman, S., and P. de Silva. 1978. Abnormal and normal obsessions. *Behaviour Research and Therapy* 16:233–48.

Salkovskis, P., R. Shafran, S. Rachman, and M. H. Freeston. 1999. Multiple pathways to inflated responsibility beliefs in obsessional problems: possible origins and implications for therapy and research. *Behaviour Research and Therapy* 37:1055–72.

Schwartz, J., and B. Beyette. 1997. *Brain Lock.* New York: Harper Perennial.

Twohig, M. P., S. C. Hayes, and A. Masuda. 2006. Increasing Willingness to Experience Obsessions: Acceptance and Commitment Therapy as a Treatment for Obsessive-Compulsive Disorder. *Behavior Therapy* 37(1):3–13

Wegner, D. 1994. *White Bears and Other Unwanted Thoughts: Suppression, Obsession, and the Psychology of Mental Control.* New York: Guilford Press.

Whitman, W. 2005. *Walt Whitman: The Complete Poems.* New York: Penguin Classics.

Yaryura-Tobias, J. A., and F. A. Neziroglu. 1997. *Biobehavioral Treatment of Obsessive-Compulsive Spectrum Disorders.* New York: W. W. Norton & Company.

Bruce M. Hyman, Ph.D., LCSW, is a Florida-licensed clinical social worker and board-certified diplomate in clinical social work who earned his master's and doctoral degrees from Florida State University. For more than twenty-four years, he has maintained an active private practice in south Florida specializing in the treatment of anxiety disorders. In 1992, he established the OCD Resource Center of Florida, which offers comprehensive services to adults and children with obsessive-compulsive disorder (OCD) and related anxiety disorders. Today, he is one of the most sought-after clinicians treating OCD and anxiety disorders in the United States. He is coauthor of *The OCD Workbook*.

Troy DuFrene is a writer who lives and works in the San Francisco Bay Area.